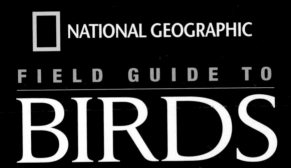

NATIONAL GEOGRAPHIC

FIELD GUIDE TO

BIRDS

D0042681

CONTENTS

6 ABOUT THIS BOOK
7 HOW TO USE THIS BOOK

11 DUCKS, GEESE
35 QUAIL
37 LOONS
41 GREBES
47 PELICANS
49 CORMORANTS
53 HERONS, EGRETS
61 VULTURES
63 HAWKS, EAGLES
75 FALCONS
77 GALLINULES, COOTS
79 PLOVERS
83 OYSTERCATCHERS
85 STILTS, AVOCETS
87 SANDPIPERS, PHALAROPES
105 GULLS, TERNS
119 PIGEONS, DOVES
123 OWLS
133 NIGHTHAWKS
135 SWIFTS
137 HUMMINGBIRDS
145 KINGFISHERS
147 WOODPECKERS

159 FLYCATCHERS
167 JAYS, CROWS
177 LARKS
179 SWALLOWS
183 CHICKADEES, TITMICE
189 NUTHATCHES
191 WRENS
203 DIPPERS
205 KINGLETS
207 THRUSHES
211 MOCKINGBIRDS, THRASHERS
215 STARLINGS
217 WAXWINGS
219 WARBLERS
233 TOWHEES, SPARROWS
245 CARDINALS
247 BLACKBIRDS, ORIOLES
259 FINCHES

262 COLOR INDEX
266 ALPHABETICAL INDEX
270 ACKNOWLEDGMENTS,
    ILLUSTRATIONS CREDITS

WELCOME TO BIRDING

I t was on Santa Cruz Island that I really became a birder. I passed a grove of oaks and spotted, foraging on the ground, the endangered Island Scrub-Jay. I rushed to check it off my life list. Then I sat—and watched. The big jay drew nearer. He perched on a fence post and looked straight at me, first with one eye, then the other. For five minutes we studied each other, the longest I had spent *looking* at a bird. I marveled at the rich purple-blue plumage, at the fearless intelligence in his eyes.

I have been birding across America for 30 years, and continue to find surprises like this everywhere I go. My bible—as it is for many—has been the *National Geographic Field Guide to the Birds of North America,* a complete field reference to the over 800 species of birds that occur on the continent.

While visiting separate regions and states, I have longed for a compact version of that guide—one I could carry in my pocket or backpack that would offer a quick reference to the birds I am most likely to see during a day in the field, and that would help birders I meet who are just getting started.

Here it is. This photographic guide to birds of California is designed to give birders of all levels an easy reference to the most commonly seen birds: What they look like at a glance, how they act, where they live, and where you can find them. The birds are listed in order of their families, as prescribed by the American Ornithologist's Union, an order used in the best field guides in the world. Before long, you will be comfortable with the family concept, and this newly acquired knowledge will aid you in your birding career. But, because finding birds *fast* is key in the field, there are two "quick reference" indexes— based on color and on alphabet.

Together, the carefully combined elements of this guide will start you on a lifelong journey of wonder and surprise.

MEL BAUGHMAN
Editor

National Geographic's *Field Guide to Birds: California* is designed to help birders at any level quickly identify birds in the field. The book is organized by bird families, following the order in the *Checklist to the Birds of North America,* by the American Ornithologists' Union. Families share structural characteristics. By learning these early, birders will establish a basis for a lifetime of identifying birds and related family members. (For quick reference in the field, use the color and alphabetical indexes at the back.)

A family may have one member or dozens of members, or species. In this book each family is identified in English, the common name. Each species is also identified in English, and by its Latin genus and species, its scientific name. One species is featured in each entry. An entry begins with Field Marks, the physical clues used to quickly identify a bird, such as body shape and size, bill length, and eye and plumage color. A bird's body parts yield vital clues to identification, so a birder needs

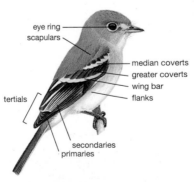

eye ring
scapulars

median coverts
greater coverts
wing bar
flanks

tertials

secondaries
primaries

Least Flycatcher

supercilium

postocular stripe

ear patch
(auricular)

moustachial stripe

submoustachial
stripe

median crown stripe

lateral crown stripe

supraloral area

lores

malar stripe

Lark Sparrow

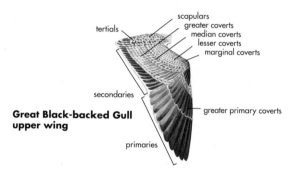

tertials

scapulars
greater coverts
median coverts
lesser coverts
marginal coverts

secondaries

greater primary coverts

**Great Black-backed Gull
upper wing**

primaries

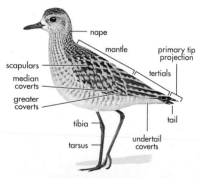

nape

mantle

scapulars

median
coverts

greater
coverts

primary tip
projection

tertials

tail

tibia

tarsus

undertail
coverts

Pacific Golden-Plover

to become familiar with them. After the first glance at body type, take note of the head shape and markings, such as stripes, eye rings, and crown. Bill shape and color are next. Then body and wing details: wing bars, color of primary flight feathers, wing color at rest, and shape and markings when extended in flight. Tail shape, length, color, and banding play a big part, too. Below is a key to using this informative guide.

❶ Beneath the **Common Name** find the **Latin**, or **Scientific, Name.** Beside it is the bird's length, and frequently wingspan. Wingspan occurs with birds often seen in flight.
❷ **Field Marks:** Gives basic field identification for body, head and bill shape, markings.
❸ **Range Map:** Shows year-round range in purple, breeding range in red, winter range in blue. Breeding colony shown by a black dot.
❹ **Behavior:** A step beyond **Field Marks,** gives clues to identifying a bird's habits, such as feeding, flight pattern, personality, courtship, nest-building, and songs and calls.
❺ **Habitat:** Reveals the area it most inhabits, such as forested regions, marshy areas, cities, or farms.

May include nesting sites.
❻ **Local Sites:** Gives the bird's ranges and local spots to look for it.
❼ **Photograph:** Shows bird in its habitat. May be a female or male adult, or a juvenile. Plumage is breeding, molting, or winter.
❽ **Caption:** Defines the featured bird's age and plumage. If a subspecies, the Latin name is given.
❾ **Field Note:** A special entry that may give a unique point of identification, or compare two species of the same family, or compare two from different families that look alike, or focus on a historic or conservation fact.
❿ **Band:** Gives the common name of the bird's family.

Year-round | Adult white morph

SNOW GOOSE

Chen caerulescens L 35" (89 cm) W 45" (114 cm)

FIELD MARKS

White overall

Black primaries

Pinkish bill with black "grinning patch"

Behavior
Often seen in huge flocks, especially during fall migration from high Arctic breeding grounds. Flocks travel in loose Vs and long lines of loud, vocal birds, sounding like baying hounds. Strong flyers, they attain speeds up to 40 mph. Known to fly over 1,500 miles nonstop. Also agile swimmers, resting mainly on water during migration and in wintering grounds.

Habitat
Seen mainly in winter on grasslands, grain fields, and coastal wetlands, preferring standing shallow fresh-water marshes and flooded fields. Almost entirely vegetarian, this goose forages on agricultural grains and plants and on all parts of aquatic vegetation.

Local Sites
Some of the country's largest flocks found in California's central valleys; others winter over in northern California's Klamath Basin area and in southern California near the Salton Sea and the Colorado River.

FIELD NOTES Look closely at individuals in a flock and you may see the diminutive Ross's Goose *Chen rossii* (inset), distinguished by a short, stubby, pinkish red bill, short neck, and round head.

Year-round | Adult *canadensis*

CANADA GOOSE

Branta canadensis L 25"-45" (64 cm-114 cm) W 50"-68" (120 cm)

FIELD MARKS

Black head and neck marked with distinctive white chin strap

In flight, shows large, dark wings, white undertail coverts, white U-shaped rump band

Pale breast color

Behavior

This most common and familiar goose is usually known for migrating in large V-formation. Its distinctive musical call of *honk-a-lonk* makes it easy to identify even without seeing it. Also makes a murmuring sound when feeding, and a hissing sound when protecting nests or young.

Habitat

Prefers wetlands, grasslands, and cultivated fields within commuting distance of water. Breeds in open or forested areas near water. It has adapted successfully to man-made habitats such as golf courses and farms, to the extent that it sometimes chases off other nesting waterbirds.

Local Sites

Common throughout California. Look for the Canada Goose in fall at Klamath Basin National Wildlife Refuge Complex and all year around in the Bay Area.

FIELD NOTES There are at least ten subspecies of Canada Goose, varying in breast coloration (inset) but generally paler in the eastern U.S., front, and darker toward the West, center. Also generally smaller in the North and West, larger in the South and East.

Breeding | Adult male

AMERICAN WIGEON

Anas americana L 19" (48 cm)

FIELD MARKS

Male's white forehead and cap
conspicuous; female's is gray

Dark green patch from eye to
nape; iridescent green speculum

Warm brown breast and sides;
white belly and rump sides; large
white patches on upper wing

Behavior

A dabbling duck, largely vegetarian and prone to
grazing, especially in fresh water, brackish marshes,
and agricultural fields. In wintering grounds, often
seen foraging on the water in mixed flocks of American
Coots and diving ducks, and known to aggressively
steal vegetation brought to the surface by the divers.
Commonly known as the "baldpate," a name coined
for the male's strikingly white forehead and crown.

Habitat

Winters throughout the northern half of the state
and along the southern coast, favoring freshwater lakes
and ponds, placid riverine environments, protected
embayments, and brackish coastal marshes.

Local Sites

Breeding populations can be found in California's
northeastern plateau region and in the Sacramento
and San Joaquin Valleys.

FIELD NOTES The American Wigeon population is increasing as
its breeding range expands eastward to the Great Lakes and to
the Maritime Provinces of Canada. Almost half of the species'
wintering population can be observed in the Pacific flyway as it
moves through California en route to Baja and mainland Mexico.

Breeding | Adult female, left; Adult male, right

MALLARD

Anas platyrhynchos L 23" (58 cm)

FIELD MARKS

Male has metallic green head, white
collar, bright chestnut breast

Female has brown mottled plumage,
orange bill marked with black

Both have white tails and underwings

Juvenile like female with olive bill

Behavior
A dabbler, it feeds by picking insects from the water's
surface or by tipping into shallows and plucking invertebrates and grasses from the bottom. The Mallard
requires no running start to take off, but springs
directly into flight. Male's courtship display includes
dipping his bill into water and bringing it up smartly.
Hybridizes with other species of dabbler, such as the
Mottled Duck and the American Black Duck.

Habitat
This wide-ranging duck nests in northern latitudes
around the globe, preferring freshwater shallows and,
in winter, salt marshes.

Local Sites
The Mallard copes well with man-made habitats and
may be found feeding in marinas and breeding in
backyards. Common throughout California year-
round. Look for the Mallard at the Don Edwards
San Francisco Bay National Wildlife Refuge.

FIELD NOTES The Mallard has two closely related cousins. One,
the Mottled Duck, *Anas fulvigula,* lives on the southern coastal
plain and does not migrate. Its plumage resembles the female
Mallard's but is darker, with an absence of white in the tail and
black on the bill.

Breeding | Adult male

CINNAMON TEAL

Anas cyanoptera L 16" (41 cm)

FIELD MARKS

Male has definitive cinnamon head, neck, and underparts

Female is mottled brown overall

Red-orange eye; long, spatulate, blackish bill

Bright blue upperwing coverts

Behavior

Small but powerful, like other dabblers, it takes flight by leaping directly into the air. Also quite agile on land, often seen running while feeding in flooded fields. Omnivorous, but favors vegetable matter. Forages mainly on vegetation and seeds. Breeding females consume small invertebrates to obtain protein required for egg laying. Less active during midday, when they rest and preen, although male will often remain alert while female sleeps.

Habitat

Prefers freshwater wetlands, including both permanent and seasonal marshes, reservoirs, slow-moving streams, cattle ponds, and even drainage ditches. Seeks emergent stands of vegetation offering cover and concealment from predators.

Local Sites

Common throughout the state, except in the desert southeast. Look for the bird in reservoirs around the state, or in marshy areas.

FIELD NOTES With the Ruddy Duck, the only duck species to breed on both North and South American continents. The North American Cinnamon Teal population is among the smallest, at 300,000 birds, but remains stable. Predation, especially among nesting birds, is high.

Breeding | Adult female, left; Adult male, right

NORTHERN SHOVELER

Anas clypeata L 19" (48 cm)

FIELD MARKS

Spatulate, grayish orange bill, longer than head

Distinctive green head in male, white breast and chestnut belly, white facial crescent in fall; female mottled brown all over

Bright orange legs and feet

Behavior

A consummate dabbler equipped with a unique bill with comblike edge that strains food items from the water. Forages while swimming, its bill submerged or skimming the surface. In shallow water, the Northern Shoveler sieves through muddy bottoms for small crustaceans and mollusks. Feeds on aquatic seeds and plants, including algae; also consumes snails and small swimming invertebrates and crustaceans. Nests in short, dense grasses near water, laying 8 to 12 eggs in a shallow scrape.

Habitat

Favors small, shallow lakes and ponds, freshwater and saline marshes, and other smaller bodies of water densely bordered by emergent vegetation.

Local Sites

Abundant and common, the Northern Shoveler winters throughout the state and breeds in the northeast and the Central Valley region. Population is expanding in the western part of the state.

FIELD NOTES With the largest bill of all North American ducks, it does not forage on land like other dabblers, but feeds only in water. Nesting females are most vulnerable to predation and will often defecate on eggs to discourage rats and mink from eating them.

Breeding | Adult male

NORTHERN PINTAIL

Anas acuta Male L 26" (66 cm) Female L 20" (51 cm)

FIELD MARKS

Chocolate-brown head, hind neck

Long white neck, breast, and underparts; thin white line behind face extending under neck

Long black central tail feathers

Female mottled brown all over

Behavior

Often seen in pairs during nesting season and in small flocks at other times, foraging in flooded agricultural fields for soybeans, corn, wheat, and rice. Also eats aquatic insects, snails, beetles, and small crustaceans. This elegant duck is an accomplished flyer known for spilling out of the sky in spectacular rapid descents.

Habitat

Frequents both freshwater and salt marshes, ponds, lakes and coastal bays. Also found in flooded agricultural environments, especially during winter. Tends to nest rather far from water on the ground, in open fields of short grass that provide little cover.

Local Sites

A widespread and abundant year-round resident of northeastern and central California, the Salton Sea vicinity, and the southwest coast. Winters throughout the state and can be found in most wetland habitats and agricultural areas.

FIELD NOTES The population has dropped by half to around three million since the 1970s. Agricultural operations destroy thousands of nests annually. Gulls, crows, and magpies prey on eggs and ducklings; Great Horned Owls and foxes on adults, especially nesting females.

Year-round | Adult male

LESSER SCAUP

Aythya affinis L 16½" (42 cm)

FIELD MARKS

Slight crown peak on black head, showing purple gloss in light

Black at tip of bill

Black neck and breast, black tail

Female has brown head, neck, upperparts; white at base of bill

Behavior

An omnivorous diving duck that forages on aquatic insects, mollusks, and crustaceans. Will dive to the bottom to sift through the mud while swimming. Also consumes snails, leeches, and small fish, and will forage for seeds and vegetation. Constructs nest near or above water and sometimes, unlike any other diver, in upland environments.

Habitat

In winter will gather in large foraging flocks on ponds, lakes, rivers, reservoirs, coastal bays, and estuaries, where it feeds mainly on mollusks, crustaceans, and insects.

Local Sites

Abundant and widespread, perhaps the most populous duck in North America, the Lesser Scaup winters throughout the state.

FIELD NOTES A close relative, the Greater Scaup, *Aythya marila* (inset), closely resembles the Lesser, with black head, neck, and breast; white center; and black tail. In good light, the more smoothly rounded head of the Greater Scaup shows a green gloss. This larger diver is seldom seen inland, instead flocking by the thousands along the coast. Both species are victims to fishing nets, but populations are large and stable.

Breeding | Adult males, left; Adult female, furthest right

SURF SCOTER

Melanitta perspicillata L 20" (51 cm)

FIELD MARKS

Male black overall, bold white
forehead and nape patch

Boldly patterned bill is red,
orange, black, and white

Distinctly sloping forehead

Female brown overall

Behavior

A true sea duck found wintering along the coast in
large flocks. Forages by diving, mainly for mollusks
such as clams and mussels. Flocks by the dozens and
more. Birds will gather in a flock in the air over a
feeding ground. The entire flock will dive at once and
then surface minutes later, several yards away. If food
is abundant, Surf Scoters will often fly back to the same
spot to repeat the feeding cycle. Bold black-and-white
head pattern earned this elegant duck the inappropri-
ate sobriquet of "skunkhead."

Habitat

Once it leaves its breeding grounds in Canada and
Alaska, the Surf Scoter moves south to the coasts to
overwinter, never leaving North America.

Local Sites

Can be seen throughout the winter along the coast,
often feeding in large flocks near rock jetties and piers.

FIELD NOTES Two other scoters share winter grounds, the White-
winged Scoter, *Melanitta fusca* (inset), which can be readily
identified by its black plumage and the white wing patch
and check mark by its eye, and the Black
Scoter, *Melanitta nigra,* an all-black
bird with a bright yellow-orange knob
on its black bill.

Breeding | Adult male

BUFFLEHEAD

Bucephala albeola L 13½" (34 cm)

FIELD MARKS

Small duck; large puffy head,
steep forehead, and short bill

Male has large white
head patch

Glossy black back

Female is duller

Behavior

Often seen in small flocks, some keeping a lookout on
the water surface while others dive for aquatic insects,
snails, and small fish. Like all divers, its feet are set well
back on the body to swiftly propel it through the water.
Migrates at night, riding favorable weather patterns.
Attains speeds of about 40 mph. A truly monogamous
duck believed to stay with the same mate for years and
faithfully return to the same nesting site each season.

Habitat

In its boreal forest breeding grounds, this smallest
of the North American diving ducks nests almost
exclusively in cavities created by the Northern Flicker—
a nesting site so tiny that it is speculated to have
influenced the Bufflehead's own small size.

Local Sites

A small inland population can be found in the Klamath
Basin of northern California, but is more abundant in
winter among coastal bays, harbors, coves, and estuaries. It prefers shallow, sheltered water.

FIELD NOTES Despite a limited breeding range and dependence
upon the Northern Flicker for nesting cavities, the Bufflehead
population is believed to have increased over the past few years.

Year-round | Adult female

Mergus serrator L 23" (58 cm)

FIELD MARKS

Dark green head, shaggy double crest in male

Bright chestnut neck, crested head in female

Long, hooded red bill and red eye

White chin, throat, and breast

Behavior

Flaps wings and runs across water or land to take off, but once airborne is a strong, swift flyer, attaining speeds near 80 mph. Rear-set legs are adapted to the aquatic life, hence it is a powerful swimmer. Uses feet to catch fish underwater. Long, thin, serrated bill grasps small fish, its principal food source. Often feeds by forming a line and herding fish cooperatively.

Habitat

Breeds in the boreal forests and tundra, preferring brackish and saltwater marshes and wetlands near the coast. Typically winters along the coasts, seeking sheltered bays, estuaries, and harbors that provide calm water in which to forage.

Local Sites

Found almost exclusively along the coast in winter, often feeding in pairs and small flocks in almost any sheltered cove, harbor, estuary, or coastal wetland.

FIELD NOTES The Common Merganser, *Mergus merganser* (inset), closely related but larger, has a blackish green head smooth in profile, a white body, and a long, slender red bill. The female has a bright chestnut neck and crested head with a white chin and breast. It winters throughout the state, both in inland waters and along the coast.

Breeding | Adult male

RUDDY DUCK

Oxyura jamaicensis L 15" (38 cm)

FIELD MARKS

Breeding male has large black head with bold white cheeks

Bright blue bill

Rusty-red body, long black tail

Female is dull brown overall

Whitish cheek, single dark line

Behavior

Referred to as a "stiff-tail" from its habit of cocking its long tail upright. This chunky diver is noted for its grebelike ability to sink beneath the surface and disappear. Adapted for diving, it has the largest feet relative to body size of all ducks. With legs positioned far back on its body, it can barely walk upright; often pushes itself along the ground. Feeds primarily on aquatic insects and other crustaceans; eats little vegetable matter.

Habitat

Breeds mainly in the Prairie Pothole region of the United States and Canada, but some populations breed throughout most of California, except in the desert.

Local Sites

In winter, found along coast and in brackish bays, marshes, and tidal estuaries. Also in freshwater marshes, ponds, and seasonally flooded croplands of the Sacramento, San Joaquin, and Imperial Valleys. Over 100,000 Ruddy Ducks overwinter on the Salton Sea.

FIELD NOTES Unlike most ducks, pair bonds form after arrival at breeding grounds and seem to last only until incubation starts. Nests are usually constructed over water in emergent vegetation. Female lays largest eggs in relation to body size of all ducks.

Year-round | Adult male *californica*

CALIFORNIA QUAIL

Callipepla californica L 10" (25 cm)

FIELD MARKS

Gray and brown above, brown sides
and crown, scaled underparts

Prominent teardrop-shaped
plume, sometimes double

Pale forehead, black throat,
white border in male

Behavior

Prefers running to flying, but will flush to escape
predators. Primarily a ground feeder, forages mainly on
seeds, flowers, buds, leaves. Will also consume spiders,
snails, beetles, and other insects. Covey members pair
up to nest. Female lays up to 20 eggs or more in nest on
ground. Precocial chicks walk and feed upon hatching.
Adult male usually acts as sentinel as the new brood
feeds. After breeding, flocks forage early morning and
late afternoon, sentinels perching on guard; generally
inactive during midday.

Habitat

This dapper New World Quail, the California state
bird, is widespread and common in open woodlands,
brushy foothills, sagebrush scrublands, and oak grasslands, usually near a permanent water source.

Local Sites

Common throughout the state, but absent from the
southeastern desert. Common at the Salton Sea
National Wildlife Refuge.

FIELD NOTES The closely related Gambel's
Quail, *Callipepla gambelii* (inset), lacks scal-
ing on underparts. It inhabits southeastern
desert scrublands and thickets with
dependable water sources. Both species visit
backyard feeding stations, swimming pools, and cattle tanks.

Breeding | Adult

COMMON LOON

Gavia immer L 32" (81 cm)

FIELD MARK

Blue-gray bill, slightly curved culmen

Steep forehead, peaked crown

Dark crown and nape, white around eye in winter

White-checked plumage, black bill during breeding

Behavior
A diving bird. Prefers fish up to 10" long, which it harpoons with its pointed beak. While swimming, keeps head level at all times. Forages by diving and swimming underwater, propelled mainly by large, paddle-shaped feet. Can stay submerged for up to three minutes at depths of up to 250 feet. It is nearly impossible for the Common Loon to walk on land. Its loud yodeling call may be heard year-round, most often on breeding grounds in spring and summer.

Habitat
Nests on large wooded lakes. Winters in coastal waters, or inland on large, ice-free bodies of water. Migrates overland as well as coastally.

Local Sites
Prefers bodies of water with ample room for takeoff. Look for it along the California coastline, particularly in the central region of the state.

FIELD NOTES In the fall, all loons abandon their northern lakes and head for warmer water. Most species of loon prefer to fly low across water while migrating, but the Common Loon flies quite high and uses slower wing beats than its relatives.

Breeding | Adult

RED-THROATED LOON

Gavia stellata L 25" (64 cm)

FIELD MARKS
Breeding adult has gray head with
brick-red throat patch

Dark brown upperparts

Lacks white patches on back
during breeding

Thin bill appears upturned

Behavior
The smallest loon, a powerful flyer, and the only loon
able to leap into flight from land or water. In flight,
neck droops below shoulders, but at rest tends to hold
head tilted up. Forages for small fish, consuming all but
largest catches underwater. Often seen hunting from
the surface by submerging its head and peering into the
water for prey as it swims.

Habitat
Breeds in high Arctic wetlands, and winters from
Alaska to northern Baja California coast, seeking pro-
tected shallow waters of bays, estuaries, and harbors.

Local Sites
Relatively common along the coast in winter, especially
in calm, protected waters, and often seen flying low
above the water, just beyond the surf. Sometimes
found on larger inland lakes, rivers,
and reservoirs.

FIELD NOTES A close relative, the Pacific
Loon, *Gavia pacifica* (inset), also has a
gray head but lacks the brick-red
throat patch and displays white spots on its back even in breeding plumage. Like other divers, loons are vulnerable to oil spills
and gill nets.

Breeding | Adult

HORNED GREBE

Podiceps auratus L 13½" (34 cm)

FIELD MARKS

Breeding adult has chestnut foreneck and golden "horns"

White cheeks and throat in winter

Dark crown and nape; lower foreneck occasionally dusky

Pale plumage in front of eyes

Behavior

Feeds by diving up to 40 feet underwater. Bone structure and position of legs further back on body assist in swimming and diving. Feeds primarily on fish and other aquatic creatures and plant matter. Seasonally monogamous, a pair will dive for food together, come up, and face one another with offerings.

Habitat

Breeds in freshwater lakes, ponds, and marshes. Winters in similar environs, as well as in saltwater areas.

Local Sites

Found in central and western California during the winter. Look for this grebe on a drive south of San Francisco on Route 1, especially around Pillar Point.

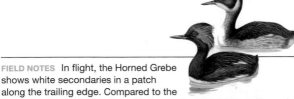

FIELD NOTES In flight, the Horned Grebe shows white secondaries in a patch along the trailing edge. Compared to the Eared Grebe, *Podiceps nigricollis* (inset), the Horned Grebe has a thicker neck and bill. Both display golden tufts and sprays that extend back from behind the eye.

Breeding | Adult

PIED-BILLED GREBE

Podilymbus podiceps L 13½" (34 cm)

FIELD MARKS

Short-necked, big-headed, stocky

Breeding adult brown overall

Black ring around stout, whitish bill

Black chin and throat

Winter birds lose bill ring,
chin becomes white

Behavior
The most secretive yet most common of North American grebes, the Pied-billed is seldom seen on land or in flight. When alarmed, it slowly sinks into the water, holding only its head above the surface. Its strong, stout bill allows it to feed on hard-shelled crustaceans, breaking apart and crushing the shells with ease. Like most grebes, it eats feathers and feeds them to its young, perhaps to protect the stomach lining from fish bones.

Habitat
Prefers nesting around freshwater marshes and ponds. Also found in more open waters of large bays and rivers, where it dives to feed on aquatic insects, small fish, frogs, and vegetable matter. Found in all of the lower 48 states.

Local Sites
Common statewide year-round except for extreme southern California, where it will winter.

FIELD NOTES There are seven species of grebe in North America, the Horned Grebe, *Podiceps auritus,* has breeding plumage distinguished by chestnut foreneck and golden "horns." It breeds on lakes and ponds, and winters on ice-free lakes. One relative, the Eared Grebe, *Podiceps nigricollis*, is a regular winter visitor to California and is found on freshwater lakes. Its winter plumage resembles the Pied-billed Grebe's.

Nonbreeding | Adult

WESTERN GREBE

Aechmophorus occidentalis L 25" (64 cm)

FIELD MARKS

Large, strikingly black and white

Long, thin neck

Black cap extends below eye

Lighter plumage around eye
in winter

Long, pointed, yellow-green bill

Behavior

Frequently seen peering into water searching for prey as it swims. Feeds almost exclusively on fish, which it pursues and often consumes underwater. Like herons, this grebe species can snap its neck instantaneously and strike or spear its prey with its long, pointed bill. In courtship, a pair will rush side by side for great distances across the surface of the water.

Habitat

Breeds mainly inland on freshwater lakes and wetlands, where emergent vegetation borders open water. A pair cooperates in building a nest over water, anchored to the vegetation. In winter, most move to coastal salt and brackish marshes, estuaries, bays, and sheltered coves, less frequently to freshwater lakes and rivers.

Local Sites

Breeds on inland lakes, marshes; and along the coast, in flocks.

FIELD NOTES Until recently the Clark's Grebe, *Aechmophorus clarkii* (inset), was considered the same species, distinguished only by its orange bill, paler back and flanks, and black cap short of the eye. In both species, female bills are shorter and smaller.

Breeding | Adult *carolinensis*

BROWN PELICAN

Pelecanus occidentalis L 48" (122 cm)

FIELD MARKS
Gray-brown body, black belly; immature bird more brown

Exceptionally long, gray bill

White head and neck, yellow wash in breeding adult; chestnut hindneck, yellow patch at base of foreneck in nonbreeding adult

Behavior
Dives from the air to capture its prey in surface water. Just before impact, its pouch balloons open, snatching up any small fish in its grasp. Some dives may be from as high as 60 feet in the air. Tilts bill down to drain water, tosses head back to swallow. Sometimes gathers in large groups over transitory schools of fish, attracting other seabirds. Flocks soar in long, staggered lines, alternately flapping and gliding in unison.

Habitat
This exclusively coastal bird makes its home along the immediate shoreline, along sheltered bays and beaches. Breeds on islands in stick nests built from materials gathered or stolen by male and presented to female.

Local Sites
Find the Brown Pelican in coastal areas from central California southward; look for it on a trip to Patrick's Point State Park.

FIELD NOTES The Brown Pelican's relative, the White Pelican, *Pelecanus erythrorhynchos* (inset), is white with a yellow crest when breeding, and an orange bill. After eggs are laid, the crest turns gray. Whites do not dive for food, but dip their bill into the water as they swim.

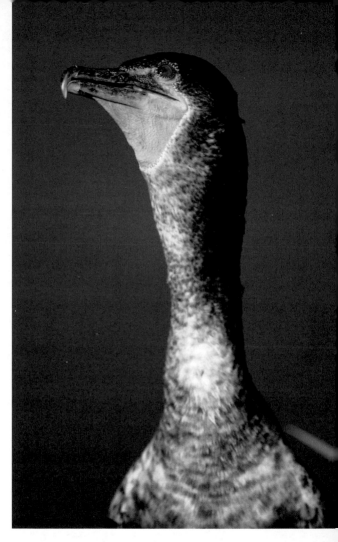

Immature | Juvenile

DOUBLE-CRESTED CORMORANT

Phalacrocorax auritus   L 32" (81 cm)   W 52" (132 cm)

FIELD MARKS

Large, rounded throat pouch yellow-orange year-round

Bill hooked at tip

In breeding adult, tuft of feathers curves back behind eyes

Distinctive kinked neck when flying

Behavior

After locating prey at surface, dives to considerable depths, propelling itself with legs and fully webbed feet. Uses its hooked bill to grasp fish. When it leaves the water, it perches on a dock or piling and half-spreads its wings to dry. Feeds on a variety of aquatic life and plants. May soar briefly at times, its neck in an S-shape. May swim submerged to the neck.

Habitat

Common and widespread, the Double-crested Cormorant may be found along coasts, inland lakes, and rivers. The most numerous and far-ranging of North American cormorants, it adapts to fresh- or saltwater environments.

Local Sites

The Double-crested Cormorant may be commonly found along the California coast year-round.

FIELD NOTES Despite its name, the crests on the head of the breeding Double-crested Cormorant are rarely seen in the field, especially in the case of the eastern breeding adult, whose crests are black and less conspicuous than the white crests of the western breeding adult. Juvenile birds are brown above, and pale below, particularly on the breast and neck.

Nonbreeding | Adult

BRANDT'S CORMORANT

Phalacrocorax penicillatus L 39" (81 cm) W 52" (132 cm)

FIELD MARKS

Black with pale buffy band of
feathers bordering throat pouch

In breeding plumage throat, or
gular, pouch becomes bright blue

Head, neck, and scapulars
acquire fine, white plumes

Behavior

Often seen flocking on fishing grounds, diving for
crabs, fish, shrimp, and the occasional squid. Strong
but not especially maneuverable in the air, the birds fly
in long lines between feeding and roosting sites, often
paralleling the coast, flying around piers and jetties,
and avoiding flying over land. Perching, one foot
usually overlaps the other. Holds wings out to dry.

Habitat

Occurs only in North America and strongly attracted
to environment along the California coast, especially
fishing grounds thick with kelp beds. A colonial nester
on offshore islands and rocky sea cliffs. Large flocks
occasionally roost at night on sandy beaches.

Local Sites

Common year-round along the coast,
usually avoiding fresh and brackish water,
preferring inshore coastal waters, bays,
lagoons, and sheltered coves.

FIELD NOTES In the Brandt's environments
you may also see the Pelagic Cormorant,
Phalacrocorax pelagicus (inset), smallest of the North Pacific
cormorants, distinguished in breeding by crown and nape tufts,
reddish face and throat patches, and white flank patches.

Nonbreeding | Adult

BLACK-CROWNED NIGHT-HERON

Nycticorax nycticorax L 25" (64 cm) W 44" (112 cm)

FIELD MARKS

Black with greenish sheen

Silvery-white spots and streaks
on wings and upper back

Long, sharply pointed bill

Buffy neck and breast
in female

Behavior

Primarily a night feeder. Even when feeding during
daylight hours, remains in the shadows, almost motionless, waiting for prey to come within range. Forages on
fish, frogs, rodents, snakes, lizards, mollusks, bird eggs,
and baby birds.

Habitat

This heron has adapted to a wide range of habitats,
including salt marshes, brackish and freshwater
wetlands, pond- and lakeshores that provide cover and
forage, along with reservoirs and flooded agricultural
fields. It finds protection from predators during
breeding season on islands and swamps.

Local Sites

Tends to concentrate in coastal wetlands, but found
throughout the western half and most of the northern
area of the state. Likely to inhabit any marsh, lake,
pond, and river environment that has forage.

FIELD NOTES Distributed worldwide, but because of its quiet,
solitary nature and nocturnal feeding habits, it is often not seen
by birders. Black-crowneds are high on the food chain and sus-
ceptible to accumulating contaminants, so their population status
is an indicator of our environmental quality. Were once considered
a food source but, like all herons, are protected today.

High Breeding | Adult male

GREEN HERON

Butorides virescens L 18" (46 cm) W 26" (66 cm)

FIELD MARKS

Small, chunky heron with short legs

Adult has deep chestnut back and sides; green and blue-gray upper-parts; white throat and neck center

Greenish-black crown feathers, sometimes raised to form a shaggy crest

Legs are dull yellow

Behavior

Usually a solitary hunter, it stalks its prey at the edge of shallow water by using twigs, insects, even earth-worms as lures and tossing them into the water to attract minnows. The Green Heron spends most of its day in the shade, but when alarmed may make a show, raising its crest, elongating its neck, and flicking its tail, in the process also revealing its lovely streaked throat plumage. This heron's common cry of *kyowk* may be heard as it flies away.

Habitat

Found in a variety of habitats, but prefers streams, ponds, and marshes with woodland cover. Often perches in trees.

Local Sites

Generally common along the coastline of the state, this small loner can be seen in the San Francisco Bay area.

FIELD NOTES Fossil specimens have indicated that the Green Heron hybridizes with the neotropical Striated Heron, a discovery that prompted their being grouped into a single species, the Green-backed Heron. It was later determined that this hybrid-ization was too infrequent to warrant the grouping, and in the 1990s, the two were resplit into separate species.

High Breeding | Adult

GREAT EGRET

Ardea alba L 39" (99 cm)

FIELD MARKS

Large white heron with heavy yellow bill, black legs and feet

Breeding adult has long plumes trailing from its back, extending beyond the tail

Duller bill and legs in nonbreeding adults and juveniles

Behavior

Stalks its prey slowly and methodically, foraging in shallow water with sharply pointed bill for small fish, aquatic insects, frogs, and crayfish. Also known to hunt snakes, birds, and small mammals. May forage in groups or steal food from smaller birds.

Habitat

Common to both fresh- and saltwater wetlands, but also feeds in open fields. The Great Egret makes its nest in trees or shrubs between 10 and 40 feet above the ground. Colonies may have one hundred birds. Occasionally breeds as far north as Canada.

Local Sites

This bird makes its year-round home in the central part of the state, but can be found in the central and northern parts of the state, from Lake Tahoe north and westward, during migration. Winters in the south near Baja California.

FIELD NOTES Early in the breeding season, the Great Egret grows long, ostentatious feathers called aigrettes. The Snowy Egret, *Egretta thula* (inset), also grows graceful plumes. In the late 1800s, the millinery industry used aigrettes so extensively that Great Egrets were hunted nearly to extinction. The campaign to end this trend became the National Audubon Society.

Nonbreeding | Adult

GREAT BLUE HERON

Ardea herodias L 46" (117 cm) W 72" (183 cm)

FIELD MARKS

Gray-blue heron, white foreneck with black streaks

Black stripe extends above eye

Breeding adult has dull yellow bill and ornate plumes on head

Juvenile has black crown, no plumes

Behavior

Often seen standing or wading along calm shorelines or rivers, foraging for food or flying high, its head folded back onto its shoulders. Emits an annoyed, deep, guttural squawk as it takes flight. When threatened, draws back its neck with plumes erect and bill pointed at opponent.

Habitat

May be seen hunting for aquatic creatures and, occasionally, snakes and insects in marshes, shores, and swamps. Farther from water, Great Blues can also be found hunting mice and small woodchucks in farm fields, meadows, and forest edges. Pairs of Great Blues build large stick nests high in trees in loose association. These "heronries" are sometimes located miles from water.

Local Sites

Winter range in California. See them at Audubon Canyon Ranch, Tule Lake National Wildlife Preserve, or Don Edwards San Francisco Bay Wildlife Reserve.

FIELD NOTES The Great Blue's relative, the Black-crowned Night Heron, *Nycticorax nycticorax,* is about half the Blue's length. It is stocky with short neck and legs. Noted by black crown, white hindneck plumes. Nests at Bodega Bay, south of Santa Rosa.

Year-round | Adult

TURKEY VULTURE

Cathartes aura L 27" (67 cm) W 69" (175 cm)

VULTURES

FIELD MARKS

Naked red head, ivory bill; red legs

Juvenile head and bill dark, legs paler

Brownish black body

Contrasting underwings show
in flight

Tail extends beyond feet in flight

Behavior

An excellent flier, the Turkey Vulture soars high above
the ground in search of carrion and refuse, watching
for other scavengers. Rocks from side to side in flight,
seldom flapping its wings, which are held up in a
shallow V, allowing it to gain lift from conditions that
would deter any other raptor. Feeds heavily when food
is available, but can go for days on nothing if necessary.

Habitat

Hunts in open country, woodland, and farmland, even
in some urban settings at dumps and landfills. Nests
solitarily in hollow logs or less frequently in hollow
trees, crevices, caves, and mine shafts.

Local Sites

Look for this bird year-round in southern and western
California. Turkey Vultures will summer in central
California. Some migrate to South America.

FIELD NOTES The Turkey Vulture's naked head is an adaptation to
keep it from soiling its feathers while feeding and therefore to
reduce the risk of picking up disease from carcasses. It also has
an unusually well-developed sense of smell, allowing it to locate
carrion concealed in forested settings.

Immature | Juvenile female

OSPREY

Pandion haliaetus L 22-25" (56-64 cm) W 58-72" (147-183 cm)

FIELD MARKS

Dark brown above, white below; female has darker neck streaks

White head, dark eye stripe, gray beak

Pale buff plumage fringe in juvenile

Wings appear bent back, slightly arched in flight

Behavior

Hunts by soaring over water, hovering, then diving down and plunging feet first into water to snatch its prey, using specialized barbs on its toes. Feeds exclusively on fish. Call is a series of clear, resonant, whistled *kyew*s, which herald the arrival of spring. The Osprey also uses its call during breeding to draw female attention to a prized fish hooked in its talons.

Habitat

Vacates the United States after breeding season, yet returns early from Central and South American wintering grounds. Nests near bodies of fresh- or saltwater. Its large, bulky nests are built up in trees or on sheds, poles, docks, or specialized man-made platforms. Uncommon inland, yet found on all continents except Antarctica.

Local Sites

The Osprey will breed in extreme northern California and will winter on the state's western edge. Look for it in the Golden Gate National Recreation area.

FIELD NOTES Females tend to be larger than males. This is an advantage for eggs, as females do the majority of brooding and supply much warmth. Also good for hatchlings, as the big female is an excellent hunter and can carry more food than the male.

Year-round | Adult

WHITE-TAILED KITE

Elanus leucurus L 16" (41cm) W 42" (107 cm)

FIELD MARKS

Long, pointed wings

Black shoulder patches, which
show in all ages as leading edges

Long, mostly white tail and underparts

Rufous streaks in juvenile on
underparts and head

Behavior

Unlike any other North American kites, hovers while
hunting, with tail down and limbs dangling, hanging
motionless in the wind like its namesake: the kite. On
sighting prey, it swoops to clutch it in its strong talons.
Feeds primarily on rodents and insects, but, not a picky
eater, uses any opportunity to catch prey. Often forms
winter roosts of more than 100 birds. Call is a brief,
whistled *keep keep keep*.

Habitat

Fairly common year-round in grasslands, farmlands,
cultivated fields, and even highway median strips. Also
makes its home in river valleys and marshes. Forms
winter roosts of over a hundred birds.

Local Sites

Look for this bird of prey along the coastline of the
state and into the central region of the state around
Sacramento.

FIELD NOTES The White-tailed Kite was once called the Black-
shouldered Kite, for its black shoulders that show in flight from
above on all ages and genders. The similar Mississippi Kite,
Ictinia mississippiensis, is distinguished by its black tail, and by
its wings that lack a black shoulder but display a white patch in
flight. The Mississippi does not hover. All kites share this: They
lack the bony ridge over the eye that other hawks exhibit.

Year-round | Adult female, left; Adult male, right

NORTHERN HARRIER

Circus cyaneus L 17-23" (43-58 cm) W 38-48" (97-122 cm)

FIELD MARKS

Owl-like facial disk

Slim body; long, narrow wings

Long tail with white uppertail coverts

Adult male grayish, white below
with chestnut spots; female brown,
white below with brown streaks

Behavior

Harriers generally perch low and fly close to the
ground, wings upraised as they search for birds, mice,
frogs, and other prey. Seldom soar high except during
migration and in exuberant acrobatic courtship
display, during which the male loops and somersaults
in the air. Often found hunting at dawn or dusk,
using well-developed hearing. During winter months,
Northern Harriers roost comunally on the ground,
alongside Short-eared Owls. Identifiable by a thin,
insistent whistle.

Habitat

Commonly called the "marsh hawk," this harrier can
often be found in wetlands and open country. Always
nests on the ground.

Local Sites

Look for the Northern Harrier in Los Banos Wildlife
Area, the San Luis National Wildlife Refuge, or the
Carrizo Plain Natural Area.

FIELD NOTES Take care when attempting to identify a Northern
Harrier high overhead. It can look like a falcon when gliding, due
to its long, broad tail, or like an accipiter when soaring, due to
its rounded wing tips. Look for its bright white rump, one of the
most noticeable field marks of any hawk.

Immature | Juvenile

GOLDEN EAGLE

Aquila chrysaetos L 30-40" (76-102 cm) W 80-88" (203-224 cm)

FIELD MARKS

Brown with yellow to tawny wash
over back of head and neck

Yellow feet, horn-colored bill

Tawny upperwing coverts

In flight, undertail shows gray to
tawny V-shaped striping

Behavior

The Golden Eagle is a true hunter and a skilled catcher
of ground squirrels, jackrabbits, and waterfowl. In
flight, wings are held slightly above the body, creating
a slight V when viewed head-on.

Habitat

Commonly associated with mountains, tundra, and
grasslands. Frequently hunts over open country. Gold-
en Eagles nest primarily on ledges and cliffs, but will
use trees on occasion.

Local Sites

Year-round resident of inland California. Look for the
Golden Eagle aloft in evenings during September and
October at the Golden Gate National Wildlife Refuge.

FIELD NOTES Although appearing similar in
size and structure, the Golden Eagle and
the Bald Eagle, *Haliaeetus leuco-
cephalus* (inset), are not closely related.
Compare the Bald Eagle's larger head, bulky bill, and shorter tail
with the Golden's sleeker body. The Bald Eagle is almost always
found near water, hunting for fish.

Year-round | Adult

COOPER'S HAWK

Accipiter cooperii L 14-20" (36-51 cm) W 29-37" (74-94 cm)

FIELD MARKS
Dark gray to black cap, bright red
to yellow eye, yellow base of bill

Blue-gray upperparts

Reddish bars across breast, belly

Long, rounded, barred tail with
white terminal band

Behavior
Usually scans for prey from a perch, then attacks with
a sudden burst of speed. Also flies fast and close to the
ground, using brush to conceal its rapid attack. Will
scan for prey while soaring. Typically feeds on birds,
rabbits, mice, ground squirrels, small reptiles, and
insects. Known to hold struggling prey underwater to
drown it. Usually consumes prey by eating it head first,
then entrails, and finally muscles.

Habitat
Prefers broken, especially deciduous, woodlands and
streamside groves. Has adapted to fragmented woodlands
created by urban and suburban development. Frequently
found in larger trees in urban woods and parks.

Local Sites
Widespread and abundant throughout the state year-
round. Less frequent in the desert southeast. Often seen
soaring overhead during spring and fall migration.

FIELD NOTES The Sharp-shinned Hawk, *Accipiter striatus,* is
a small version of the Cooper's, with a proportionally smaller
head and a more squared-off tail. Can be distinguished in
flight, since the Sharp-shinned's head appears to be pulled
into the shoulders.

Year-round | Adult rufous morph *calurus*

RED-TAILED HAWK

Buteo jamaicensis L 22" (56 cm) W 50" (127 cm)

FIELD MARKS

Brown body, heavy beak

Distinctive red tail

Whitish belly with dark streaks

Dark bar on leading edge of underwing

Juvenile has gray-brown tail

Behavior

While searching for prey, the Red-tailed Hawk hovers in place, sometimes kiting, or hanging motionless in the wind, as it scours the land. It preys on rodents. Listen for its distinctive call, a harsh, descending *keeeeeer*.

Habitat

Variable habitat, from woods with nearby open lands to plains, prairie groves, and even deserts. Scan for hawks along edges where fields meet forests, or where wetlands meet woodlands—favored habitats due to the variety of prey found there.

Local Sites

The Lower Klamath and Tule Lake National Wildlife Refuges are home to nesting Red-Taileds in the spring and summer. Then look for their southward migration in the fall from the Golden Gate National Recreation Area.

FIELD NOTES Variable pale and dark feathers on mantle form a broad V, visible on perched birds. The related Red-shouldered Hawk, *Buteo elegans* (inset), is a slightly smaller bird. It has spotted brown plumage with reddish shoulders, wing linings, and chest; a long tail with broad white tail bands; and long, golden-yellow legs.

Year-round | Adult

AMERICAN KESTREL

Falco sparverius L 10½" (27 cm) W 23" (58 cm)

FIELD MARKS
Russet back and tail

Two black stripes on white face

Male has blue-gray wing coverts
and row of white spots on trailing
edge of wing

Female has russet wing coverts

Behavior

Feeds on insects, reptiles, mice, and other small
mammals, often hovering over prey before plunging.
Will also feed on small birds, especially in winter. Regularly seen perched on telephone lines, frequently bobbing its tail. Has clear call of *killy killy killy.*

Habitat

The most widely distributed falcon, the American
Kestrel is commonly seen in open country and in cities.
Can often be found mousing in highway
medians or sweeping down the surf line.

Local Sites

Common throughout California year round. May be
seen perching on telephone wires, or on city
buildings.

FIELD NOTES A related species, the Peregrine Falcon, *Falco peregrinus* (inset),
sports a distinctive black helmet, has a
rufous breast spotted with brown, and has
white and brown legs and tail. The Peregrine feeds primarily on
birds and is often seen in an urban environment, perching on tall
buildings. The Prairie Falcon, *Falco mexicanus* , is slightly larger
in size, with pale brown above, creamy white and spotted below.
The Prairie's crown is streaked, and its white face and neck have
vertical brown stripes below and behind the eye.

Year-round | Adults

AMERICAN COOT

Fulica americana L 15½" (39 cm)

FIELD MARKS

Blackish head and neck

Small, reddish brown forehead

Whitish bill with dark band at tip

Slate body

Outer feathers of undertail coverts white, inner black

Behavior

The distinctive toes of the American Coot are flexible and lobed, permitting this bird to swim well in open water and even dive in pursuit of aquatic vegetation beneath the surface. Coots are the only rails with the ability to stay submerged to feed. They bob their small heads back and forth when walking or swimming and may be seen foraging in large flocks, especially during the winter. Note leg color, which ranges from green in juveniles to yellow in adults.

Habitat

Nests in freshwater marshes and wetlands, or near lakes and ponds. Winters in both fresh- and salt water. Has also adapted well to human-altered habitats, including pits and sewage lagoons for foraging, and suburban lawns for resting.

Local Sites

Common and abundant throughout California.

FIELD NOTES The Common Moorhen, *Gallinula chloropus* (inset), can be distinguished from the American Coot by its red forehead shield, brownish olive back, slate underparts, and white streaking on its flanks.

Breeding | Adult male

BLACK-BELLIED PLOVER

Pluvialis squatarola L 11½" (29 cm) W 45"

FIELD MARKS

Roundish head and body, dark legs

Large eyes, short bill

Breeding male has frosted crown and nape, white belly

Breeding female similar, but with less black

Behavior

In small, loose groups, hunts for invertebrates such as small mollusks, worms, shrimp, insects, small crabs, along with eggs and sometimes berries. Locates prey by sight, darting across the ground, then stops, then runs off again. In this respect, plovers have a similar hunting style to that of the American Robin or other thrushes. Listen for the Black-bellied Plover's drawn-out three-note whistle, the second note lower in pitch.

Habitat

This shorebird prefers sandy shores and beaches. Nests on the Arctic tundra. Is rare in interior regions.

Local Sites

Winters along the entire coastline of California, from Patrick's Point State Park in the north, to Tijuana Slough National Wildlife Reserve in the south.

FIELD NOTES Plovers are swift flyers, due in part to their long, pointed wings. While observing their aerial acrobatics, watch for black axillaries, white uppertail coverts, and the barred white tail. Females are similar to males in all types of plumage, except that their plumage appears to include less black. In winter, the adult's plumage—and plumage of all juveniles—appears mottled gray with white belly. Note that juveniles of the species may be gold-speckled above.

Year-round | Adult

KILLDEER

Charadrius vociferus L 10½" (27 cm)

FIELD MARKS

Tan to chocolate-brown above, white neck and belly

Black, double breast bands

Black stripe on forehead and extending back from black bill

Reddish eye ring

Behavior

Well-known for feigning a broken wing when predators come near its nest, it will limp to one side, drag its wing, and spread its tail. Once intruders depart from the nest, the instantly "healed" Killdeer will take flight, and can then be identified by its reddish orange rump. Is often seen running, then stopping on a dime with an inquisitive look, then suddenly jabbing at the ground with its bill. May gather in loose flocks. Feeds mainly on insects found in short vegetation.

Habitat

Although a type of plover, a shorebird, the Killdeer prefers interior grassy regions, but may also be found on shores. In summer, it can be found across the entire continent of North America south of the tundra. Builds nests on open ground, usually on gravel.

Local Sites

Common through California year-round and may be found in fallow fields, city parking lots, golf courses, and other areas in close proximity to humans.

FIELD NOTES The Killdeer's loud, piercing, eponymous call, *kill-dee,* or its ascending *dee-dee-dee* is often a way to identify the bird before actually sighting it. Listen also for a long, trilled *trrrrrrr* during courtship displays or when a nest is threatened by a predator.

Year-round | Adult

BLACK OYSTERCATCHER

Haematopus bachmani L 17½" (45 cm)

FIELD MARKS

Black to blackish brown plumage overall

Bright orange eye ring, yellow iris

Long, red-orange bill

Pinkish legs

Behavior

The only uniformly blackish shorebird in North America. Feeds heavily on mussels, limpets, chitons, and occasionally on sea urchins or crabs, not oysters, despite its name. When bivalves part their shells, it quickly inserts its bill, cuts the muscle, and feeds on the soft parts. Pairs are monogamous, known to use the same nest site for years. The nest is made of shell fragments and small stones, mainly collected by the male and formed into a shallow depression.

Habitat

Found only in the marine shoreline environment, favoring rocky over sandy areas. Breeds mainly on mixed sand and gravel shelves of rocky islands and headlands, just above the intertidal zone.

Local Sites

Relatively tame, it is easily found year-round along the entire California coast, especially along rocky stretches.

FIELD NOTES After breeding, loose flocks form and roost communally above the tidal surge. Migration is believed to be minimal in California populations, though you may see flocks in long lines beyond the surf, traveling from roost sites to feeding areas. Urban sprawl and other disturbances cause oystercatchers to abandon breeding areas for years, if not permanently.

Nonbreeding | Adult male

AMERICAN AVOCET

Recurvirostra americana L 18" (46 cm)

FIELD MARKS

Striking black and white plumage;
white belly; head gray in winter,
rust-colored when breeding

Long, bluish legs and feet

Sharply recurved bill, longer and
straighter in males

Behavior

Feeds by walking in a loose line, sweeping its slightly
open bill, scythelike, through the water, searching the
bottom for fish and invertebrates. Will also feed on
larvae of insects, on small crustaceans, and on other
invertebrates.

Habitat

A graceful wader, it prefers coastal areas, alkaline
lakes, and briny ponds for foraging. Avocets are very
tolerant of cold and will even winter in icy conditions.

Local Sites

Look for the American Avocet year-round in interior
areas of the state, from the Tule Lake National Wildlife
Refuge south toward the Carrizo Plain Natural Area.
Will winter along the coastline, from south of San
Francisco Bay toward Santa Barbara.

FIELD NOTES Juvenile American Avocets have a gray face and
a cinnamon wash on their heads and necks. Compare the
American Avocet with the Black-necked Stilt, *Himantopus
mexicanus*, which has long, red-orange legs, a glossy black bill,
and white underparts. Males are dark black from the top of the
head and cheeks, down the back to the tail. Females and
juvenile Black-necked Stilts are dark brown.

Breeding | Adult *inornatus*

WILLET

Catoptrophorus semipalmatus L 15" (38 cm)

FIELD MARKS

Large and plump with long gray legs

Breeding adult is heavily mottled with white belly

Winter plumage pale gray above

In flight, shows black-and-white wing pattern with black edges

Behavior

The Willet, like other shorebirds, wades through the water in search of prey, probing through mud with its long bill. Feeds primarily on aquatic insects and their larvae. Forages on land for seeds and rice as well. Its call of *pill-will-willet* can be heard commonly on breeding grounds. Also gives a *kip-kip-kip* call when alarmed. As protective as they are, Willets are known to leave unhatched eggs behind once the first young leaves the nest. A Willet sleeps on one leg, with head tucked in on its back.

Habitat

Nests in wetlands during the spring and summer months, usually within 200 feet of another Willet nest. Moves closer to the coastline in winter. Look for the juvenile, which is mottled golden-brown.

Local Sites

Winters along the coastline of California, particularly in the central part of the state, around the San Francisco Bay area.

FIELD NOTES During courtship displays, the Willet will show its black-and-white underwing patches, one of the more identifiable field marks of this otherwise fairly nondescript bird. Keep an eye out as well for the white tail and rump.

Nonbreeding | Adult

GREATER YELLOWLEGS

Tringa melanoleuca L 14" (36 cm)

FIELD MARKS
Long, bright yellow legs
Long, dark, slightly upturned bill
Long, slender neck
White-speckled, gray-brown back
White underparts

Behavior
Usually seen alone or in small groups, this wary bird
sounds an alarm when a hawk or falcon approaches.
Call is distinctive series of three or more descending
tew tew tew sounds. A forager of snails, crabs, and
shrimp; also skims water surface for insects and larvae.
Sprints short distances in pursuit of small fish

Habitat
Breeds throughout the Canadian boreal zone, then
winters throughout coastal North America and south
into Mexico, utilizing a full range of wetlands, including marshes, ponds, lakes, rivers, and reservoirs.

Local Sites
Among the most common shorebirds; especially favors
coastal marshes, mudflats, and estuaries in winter.

FIELD NOTES The Lesser Yellowlegs, *Tringa flavipes* (inset), a very
close relative, shares winter coastal habitats. Distinguished by
its shorter bill—no longer than the depth of the head—it is smaller in stature and much less wary in behavior. The Lesser's call is
often a single or double *tew*. Yel-
lowlegs were once a favored bird for
market hunters, so their populations
were greatly diminished by the early
1900s. Today protected, their populations are stable.

Year-round | Adult

LONG-BILLED CURLEW

Numenius americanus L 23" (58 cm)

FIELD MARKS

Very long, strongly downcurved bill

Pinkish to grayish brown base of lower mandible

Cinnamon-brown above, buff-brown underparts

Long, bluish gray legs

Behavior

Largest North American shorebird. Named for its loud, musical, ascending *cur-lee* call. Bill adapted for probing tidal mudflats for shrimp and crabs and soggy fields for earthworms. Also feeds on insects, larvae, mollusks, crustaceans, and small amphibians. The female usually abandons the nest two to three weeks after hatching, when the male takes over brood care.

Habitat

Breeds in grasslands of western U.S. and southwestern Canada. Seldom travels more than 1,500 miles from its interior nesting grounds to winter from the Central Valley and Pacific coastline of California into Mexico.

Local Sites

Infrequent on the north coast, but common in winter along the coast and in Central Valley's rice-growing areas, managed wetlands, pasturelands, and evaporation and sewerage ponds.

FIELD NOTES The Whimbrel, *Numenius phaeopus* (inset), a close relative, shares the winter coast habitat, and is distinguished by its overall smaller size and sharply defined pale eye stripe, dark eye line, and boldly striped crown.

Nonbreeding | Adult

MARBLED GODWIT

Limosa fedoa L 18" (46 cm)

FIELD MARKS

Tawny brown, mottled with black above; cinnamon shows in flight

Finely barred buff-brown underparts

Long, slightly upcurved, bicolored bill

Long bluish gray legs

Behavior
Named for its loud call, *godWIT godWIT.* Flight is strong and swift, bill pointing straight ahead and long legs trailing behind. Uses bill to probe for worms, mollusks, and small crustaceans. Will glean insects from vegetation, and small fish from shallows. Tends to nest in large, loose colonies with no clearly defined territories. Hides nests well in prairie grasses, and is reluctant to flush even when closely approached.

Habitat
Breeds in the prairies of northern U.S. and southern Canada, where it feeds on insects, including grass-hoppers, and worms, seeds, and berries. In winter favors tidal mudflats, coastal estuaries, sandy beaches, meadows, and farm fields.

Local Sites
Large wintering flocks are common along the coast from San Francisco Bay south. Small populations are near Sacramento, and at Salton Sea National Wildlife Refuge.

FIELD NOTES Once highly prized for the restaurant trade, until hunting for shorebirds was outlawed in 1916. Since then, much of the Godwit's prairie nesting habitat has been converted to farmland, contributing to its further decline.

Nonbreeding | Adult

Arenaria melanocephala L 9¼" (24 cm)

FIELD MARKS

Gray-black upperparts, head, neck

Black bill with slightly upturned tip

Breeding plumage shows white spot in front of eye

White belly

Behavior

Blends well with rocky shoreline habitat; almost impossible to see until it moves. Walks and hops around rocks, using wedge-shaped bill to turn shells and stones, as it forages for insects. Also feeds on barnacles, crustaceans, and mollusks, using bill to pry open shells, and to remove food from rocks. Known to eat small bird eggs and carrion. Nest site is barely a scrape on the ground, formed mainly by the male and used in successive seasons. Call is a guttural rattle.

Habitat

Breeds in coastal Alaska just above the high-tide mark. Winters along Pacific Coast from southern Alaska to the Baja Peninsula. Believed to migrate during the day in small, compact flocks flying well offshore.

Local Sites

Abundant on coast, especially at Bodega Head and Doran County Park, north of San Francisco.

FIELD NOTES Both the Black Turnstone and its cousin, the Ruddy Turnstone, *Arenaria interpres* (inset), have complex wing patterns in flight. The breeding Ruddy has black and chestnut back.

Nonbreeding | Adult

SANDERLING

Calidris alba L 8" (20 cm)

FIELD MARKS

In winter pale gray above, white below

Bill and legs black

Prominent white wing stripe

Head, mantle, and breast rusty in breeding plumage

Behavior

Feeds on sandy beaches, chasing retreating waves to snatch up newly exposed mollusks and crustaceans. Stands on one leg for a long period of time, even though it lacks a hind toe. An excellent flyer, aided by an ample wing length and sharp, pointed wings. Prominent white wing stripe shows especially in flight. Flock will wheel and turn in tandem in the air. Breeding plumage not acquired until late April. Call is a sharp *kip*, often emitted in a series.

Habitat

Breeds on tundra in the remote Arctic and sub-Arctic, west from Hudson Bay. Migrates in the winter to sandy beaches throughout most of the Southern Hemisphere, traveling as far as 8,000 miles.

Local Sites

Look for the Sanderling in winter, feeding along the entire coast. One spot is McGrath State Beach.

FIELD NOTES Small shorebirds like the Sanderling are known as "peeps," after their calls. The plumage of the Sanderling (inset) is dramatically brighter during breeding season, at right, than in winter, when its pale gray blends in with its sandy environment.

Breeding | Adult

LEAST SANDPIPER

Calidris minutilla L 6" (15 cm)

FIELD MARKS

Short, thin, slightly decurved bill

Brown-gray upperparts

Dark streaked neck and breast, strong buff wash across juvenile breast

White belly and undertail coverts

Yellowish to greenish legs

Behavior

Often looks as if it is chasing waves as it forages for food with its stout, spiky bill. Feeds on a wide variety of invertebrates, such as worms, insects, mollusks, small crabs, and fish, in muddy, sandy, or shallow water. Also is known to feed in newly plowed agricultural fields. The Least Sandpiper's call is characterized by a high *kree*. In nesting areas, it may confuse predators with a "rodent-run" display in which its feathers puff out, its wings droop, and the bird runs along the ground, squeaking like a rodent.

Habitat

Common in coastal tidal regions and in wetlands with exposed mud, sand, rock, and short grasses. Breeds in Arctic regions.

Local Sites

Seen along the coastline and in interior near Salton Sea in winter.

FIELD NOTES The smallest North American sandpiper closely resembles the Western Sandpiper, *Calidris mauri* (inset). This species has a slightly larger, tapered bill, arrow-shaped spots on sides, rufous wash on back, crown and ear patches, and black legs and feet.

Nonbreeding | Adult male

LONG-BILLED DOWITCHER

Limnodromus scolopaceus L 11½" (29 cm)

FIELD MARKS

Long, straight, dark bill

Very pale chin and eye stripe

Dark centered feathers on back with bold white edge

Dark barring on throat, breast, and belly; reddish below

Behavior

Tactile feeder; hunts worms, insects, mollusks, small crabs, and fishes by probing the water with rapid jabbing motion, much like a sewing machine. Call is a sharp, high-pitched *keek,* given singly or in a rapid series. Juveniles migrate later than adults and are generally lighter in color.

Habitat

Prefers water habitats with shallow or muddy water.

Local Sites

Common in migration throughout the western half of the North American continent. Prefers to winter along the entire California coastline.

FIELD NOTES The Short-billed Dowitcher, *Limnodromus griseus* (inset), is a half-inch smaller than the Long-billed Dowitcher, but bill sizes of the two are about the same, and similar coloration also makes it difficult to tell them apart. The Short-billed Dowitcher appears to have more yellowish tones between the black spots on its back. The Short-billed call is a mellow *tu tu tu,* repeated in a rapid series if alarmed. In flight, both species of dowitchers show a white wedge from their barred tails to the middle of their backs. Their greenish yellow legs and feet just barely extend beyond their tails in flight.

Breeding | Adult female

RED-NECKED PHALAROPE

Phalaropus lobatus L 7¾" (20 cm)

FIELD MARKS

Black face and crown

White spot in front of eye

Breeding female shows chestnut pattern on front and sides of neck

Chestnut pattern and overall coloring muted in male

Behavior

Spins in a tight circle on the water, creating a small vortex to concentrate the zooplankton on which it feeds. Roles are reversed in the domestic lives of the phalarope. Only the male has a brood patch for incubating eggs, and he is less colorful than the female. When incubation begins, the flashy female leaves the relationship, often to breed with another male. Call is a series of high-pitched, sharp *kit* notes.

Habitat

Generally pelagic, but common inland and off the coast during migration. Breeds on the Arctic and subarctic tundra. Winters chiefly at sea in the Southern Hemisphere.

Local Sites

Seen feeding along shoreline, turning stones in its search for small mollusks and crustaceans.

FIELD NOTES Relative of the Red-necked Phalarope, the Wilson's Phalarope *Phalaropus tricolor* (inset), is chiefly an inland bird. It frequents marshes and wetlands, where it feeds on insects, larvae, and seeds, and also probes the mud flats for small crustaceans.

Nonbreeding | Adult

HEERMANN'S GULL

Larus heermanni L 19" (48 cm) W 51" (130 cm)

FIELD MARKS

White head, streaked gray-brown in winter

Red bill with black tip

Dark eye with red orbital ring

Dark gray upperparts, pale gray underparts and breast

Behavior

Spends most of its time in the air. Can be identified overhead by its black tail with white terminal band. It plunge-dives for fish and also forages for crustaceans, clams, insects, and eggs and chicks from other birds. Walking on its blue-gray legs and feet, it will gather near feeding seals, sea otters, and flocks of pelicans and cormorants, often stealing a catch from the unwary, or feeding on discarded food items.

Habitat

This coastal bird spends most of its time over the water and very little time on the beach.

Local Sites

A common postbreeding visitor along the state's western coast, though very rare at Salton Sea. It does wander inland but is rarely seen there.

FIELD NOTES The white head, overall dark body, and bright red bill distinguish the Heerman's Gull from all other gulls, since it is the only gull that diverges from the typical plumage pattern of light below and dark above. Young Heerman's Gulls are overall brown with a yellow-orange bill with black tip. As they mature, they become progressively more gray in color.

Breeding | Adult

BONAPARTE'S GULL

Larus philadelphia L 13½" (34 cm) W 33" (84 cm)

FIELD MARKS

Black bill; gray mantle

Breeding adult has black hood, absent in winter adult

Black wingtips, pale on underside; white underparts

Orange-red legs

Behavior

Among the smallest of North American gulls, it breeds in northern boreal coniferous forests. Mainly nests in trees, one of the only gulls to do so. Constructs cup nest of twigs and bark lined with moss and lichens. Feeds on insects during breeding season. Favors marine environment during winter, where it often forages in large flocks by plunge-diving and skimming for small fish and shrimp.

Habitat

Common and abundant along the coast in winter, sometimes feeding several miles offshore. Will gather at river mouths during salmon runs, feeding on small fish and salmon eggs.

Local Sites

Winters along the entire California coast, favoring the pure marine environment, and on tidal mudflats.

FIELD NOTES Named after Charles Lucien Bonaparte, a nephew of Napoleon, the Bonaparte's Gull is one of the most graceful gulls in flight. A ferocious defender of its nest, it often flies several hundred yards to assault intruders, including humans. Though it is omnivorous and willing to forage on a variety of prey, it seldom feeds at garbage dumps, unlike most other gulls.

Breeding | Adult *brachyrhynchus* with chick

MEW GULL

Larus canus L 16" (41 cm) W 43" (109 cm)

FIELD MARKS

White head, neck, breast,
and underparts

Large, dark eyes

Small yellow bill

Gray mantle

Greenish yellow legs and feet

Behavior

A western gull, it breeds in Alaska and the Canadian
Yukon, then migrates south along the coast during
winter. Uses a range of habitats: inland freshwater lakes,
ponds, marshes, rocky shores, and tundra. The only
white-headed gull to nest in trees. Forages on crayfish,
fish, insects, worms, carrion, and garbage. Spins in tight
circles over water like a phalarope, feeding on small
food items stirred up by the motion.

Habitat

Frequents a full range of habitats, especially during
breeding season, from coastline to salt marshes, lakes,
ponds, rivers, bays, and estuaries. Favors the coast during
winter, but seldom moves more than a mile offshore.

Local Sites

Widespread and abundant in winter along the entire
California coast. Frequents sewerage ponds, garbage
dumps, and agricultural fields. Often follows farm
machinery, feeding on exposed insects and worms.

FIELD NOTES Smallest of North America's white-headed gulls,
this adaptable bird has a worldwide distribution of over one
million breeding pairs—over 100,000 in Alaska alone. It perches
atop trees and sounds out its melancholy, catlike *mee-you* call.

Breeding | Adult

CALIFORNIA GULL

Larus californicus L 21" (53 cm) W 54" (137 cm)

FIELD MARKS

White head, heavily streaked with brown in winter; white underparts

White neck and breast; gray back

Yellow bill with black and red spots on lower mandible

Black primaries with white spots

Behavior

Forages on insects, rodents, eggs and chicks, refuse, and carrion. This species of gull saved the Mormon settlement in Utah by consuming the hordes of grasshoppers that swarmed their agricultural fields. The California Gull is the Utah state bird.

Habitat

Found primarily inland during summer, moving to the coast during the winter.

Local Sites

Look for this gull year-round in the San Francisco Bay region and in interior regions around Lake Tahoe. In the winter, it will commonly be seen along the entire Pacific coast of California.

FIELD NOTES The pale gray Herring Gull, *Larus argentatus* (inset)—with its yellow bill with the bright red spot—and the Western Gull, *Larus occidentalis*—with a much darker gray-black back and bright yellow bill with a red spot—share the California coast with the California Gull. Juveniles of each species appear the same, having mottled brown plumage with darker brown tails. But the Herring Gull juvenile is a paler brown, and the Western Gull juvenile is darker.

Immature | Second-winter

RING-BILLED GULL

Larus delawarensis L 17½" (45 cm) W 48" (122 cm)

FIELD MARKS

Yellow bill with black
subterminal ring

Pale eye with red orbital ring

Black primaries showing white spots

Pale gray upperparts,
white underparts

Behavior

This vocal gull is heard calling to other gulls, especially during feeding and nesting. It calls, croaks, and cries incessantly. The call consists of a series of laughing croaks that begins with a short, gruff note and falls into a series of *kheeyaahhh* sounds. This opportunistic feeder will scavenge for seeds, grains, grasses, fish, fruit, dead fish, and marine invertebrates.

Habitat

Primarily a coastal bird. Will nest in interior regions, but the gulls space themselves out along the coastline for the winter.

Local Sites

Abundant and widespread throughout the winter months, the Ring-Billed Gull is usually spotted along the coastline. Look for it at Golden Gate Park.

FIELD NOTES Gulls breed on the ground, often in large colonies that can include several species. Even when female Ring-billed Gulls are successful in mating, they may be unable to find a mate. To assure care of their fledglings, they have been observed to tend nests in pairs or trios. The scarcity of breeding males may be a result of differing survival rates, but in some cases reduced numbers were known to be a consequence of DDT use in an area.

Breeding | Adults, foreground; Juvenile, background right

CASPIAN TERN

Sterna caspia L 21" (53 cm) W 50" (127 cm)

FIELD MARKS

Large, thick, coral-red bill

Pale gray with white underparts

Black cap extends bill to nape
and drops below eye

In flight, shows dark underside of
primaries and slightly forked tail

Behavior

Often hovers before plunge-diving for small fish, its
principle food source. Also sits gull-like and feeds from
the water's surface. This largest tern is quite predatory
in nature, frequently stealing catches from other gulls
and terns and feeding on their eggs and chicks. Forms
monogamous pair bonds and usually nests in colonies.
Adult's calls include a harsh *kowk* and *ca-arr*. Immature
Caspian Tern whistle is *whee-you*.

Habitat

More common along the coast, but also a regular
visitor to inland lakes and wetlands.

Local Sites

Breeds around San Francisco area. Winters
to the south. Look for it there, around
Morro Bay and Montana de Oro State
Parks, and south to Los Angeles.

FIELD NOTES Compare the Caspian with the Royal
Tern, *Sterna maxima*, with its smaller, orange bill,
and the Elegant Tern, *Sterna elegans* (inset), with its stiletto-like,
reddish orange bill and large black cap and crest. Both species
share the coast with the Caspian Tern.

Breeding | Adult

FORSTER'S TERN

Sterna forsteri L 14½" (37 cm)

FIELD MARKS
Black cap and nape on breeding adult

Orange-red bill with dark tip

Pale gray upperparts

Snow-white underparts

Orange legs and feet

Behavior
When feeding, the Forster's flies back and forth over the water. May forage on insects, picking them from the water's surface. Also plunge-dives to capture small fish. Often gives a one-note call while feeding over water, or during breeding season, especially a hoarse *kyarr*. Migrates to the Midwest, Pacific Northwest, and southern Canada to breed.

Habitat
Has large wintering range in the United States, mainly coastal, along the Gulf and portions of the East and West Coasts. Also inhabits inland marshes and lakes where abundant fish and insects might be found.

Local Sites
Breeding range extends from San Francisco Bay, northward to Tule Lake National Wildlife Refuge, and southward to Lake Tahoe. Find Forster's Terns during the winter months along the coastline.

FIELD NOTES Terns mate in monogamous pair bonds, which are formed in ritualized calling and aerial displays, initiated by the male landing near a female and offering her a fish. Parents in a colony defend their young by screeching and diving at intruders.

Year-round | Adult wildtype

ROCK PIGEON

Columba livia L 12½" (32 cm)

FIELD MARKS

Highly variable, multicolored

Head and neck usually darker than back

White rump

Dark band at end of tail

Black bars on inner wing

Behavior

Feeds during the day on grain, seeds, fruit, or refuse in parks and fields. Frequently visits backyard feeding stations. As pigeons forage, they move with a short-stepped, stodgy gait—"pigeon-toed"—while their heads bob fore and aft. Characterized by soft *coo-cuk-cuk-cuk-coooo* call. In courtship display, male turns in circles while cooing. Courtship can result in a pairing for life. Nest is built of stiff twigs, sticks, leaves, and grasses.

Habitat

Widespread throughout United States. Nests and roosts primarily on high window ledges, in and on bridges, and in barns.

Local Sites

Look for the Rock Pigeon throughout the state, in urban parks, country fields, and wherever someone is willing to spread bread crumbs or seeds.

FIELD NOTES Distinguish a flock of Rock Pigeons in flight from a flock of Band-tailed Pigeons, *Columba fasciata,* by the variety of plumage the Rocks show. Colors range from rust red to multi-colors. The colors developed over centuries of near domestication. Those resembling their wild ancestors have head and neck darker than back, a white rump, and a black band at end of tail.

Year-round | Adult female

Zenaida macroura L 12" (31 cm)

FIELD MARKS

Small, pinkish head with black spot on lower cheek; pinkish wash below

Trim-bodied, with long tail tapering to a point

Brownish-gray upperparts, black spots on upper wings

Behavior

Generally a ground feeder, a Mourning Dove will forage for grains and other seeds, grasses, and insects. Known for its mournful call, *oowooo-woo-woo-woo*, sometimes repeated several times. Wings produce a fluttering whistle as the bird takes flight. A very successful breeder, a Mourning Dove may have several broods during a breeding season, each one consisting of two or three chicks.

Habitat

Found in a variety of habitats, the Mourning Dove prefers an open setting, often choosing urban or suburban sites for feeding and nesting, including front porch eaves.

Local Sites

This is the most abundant and widespread dove. It is easily spotted throughout California year-round.

FIELD NOTES Barely half the size of the Mourning Dove, the Common Ground-Dove *Columbina passerina* (inset), measures only 6¹/₄" (17 cm). Found in the brushy scrublands of southern California, it is readily identified by its bright chestnut primaries and wing linings visible in flight. The plumage on its head and chest have a heavily scaled appearance.

Year-round | Adult male

BARN OWL

Tyto alba L 16" (41 cm)

FIELD MARKS

Definitive white heart-shaped face

Dark eyes

Rusty-brown above, cinnamon-barred back

White to pale-cinnamon underparts

Behavior

Nocturnal forager of mice and small birds, primarily hunting by sound. Fluffy plumage makes its flight almost soundless, effective in surprising its prey. Uses one upward-pointing and one downward-pointing ear to search for bats, snakes, and mice, which it catches in its talons. Roosts and nests in dark cavities in city and farm buildings, cliffs, and trees.

Habitat

Distributed throughout the world, this owl has adapted to the activities of man and is found in urban, suburban, farmland, and forest regions throughout its range. Nests are built in various sites, including tree hollows, barn rafters, burrows, or cliff holes.

Local Sites

A year-round resident of California. To find an owl, search the ground for regurgitated pellets of fur and bone below a nest or roost. Listen for flocks of small songbirds noisily mobbing a roosting owl.

FIELD NOTES Farmers enjoy the presence of these owls because they are such efficient mousers. They nest at all times of the year and, it is believed, mate for life. Note that the darkest birds are always females.

Year-round | Adult

SHORT-EARED OWL

Asio flammeus L 15" (38 cm)

FIELD MARKS

Dark facial disk with pale edges

Yellow to yellow-orange eyes

Tawny plumage overall

Boldly streaked breast, paler belly

In flight, long wings show buffy patch above, black wrist below

Behavior

Long, broad wings make this owl a graceful flyer, able to hover even on windless days, and often seen soaring. Primarily a nocturnal hunter of small mammals, especially voles, its population correlates directly to the abundance of available prey. Very regularly hunts in daytime over open fields, and will occasionally add small birds and large insects to its menu.

Habitat

Favors grasslands, marshes, fields, and prairies. It is believed that as food becomes more scarce, the Short-eared Owl is forced to spend more time hunting, and is thus more likely to be seen during daylight hours with the approach of late fall and winter.

Local Sites

Common in northern California year-round; moves south throughout the state during the winter.

FIELD NOTES A relative, the Long-eared Owl, *Asio otus* (inset), is more nocturnal and less likely to be seen in daylight. Where their ranges overlap, in the Central Valley and on the southern coast, they often roost in the same area.

Year-round | Adult

GREAT HORNED OWL

Bubo virginianus L 22" (56 cm)

FIELD MARKS
Large overall size
Long ear tufts (or "horns")
Rusty facial disks
Yellow eyes
White chin and throat

Behavior
Chiefly nocturnal, feeds on a wide variety of animals including cats, skunks, porcupines, birds, snakes, grouse, and frogs. Watches from high perch, then swoops down on prey. Call is a series of three to eight loud, deep hoots, the second and third hoots often short and rapid. The Great Horned Owl may be the earliest bird to nest each year, beginning in early January or February, possibly to take advantage of winter-stressed prey.

Habitat
The most widespread owl in North America, the Great Horned Owl can be found in a wide variety of habitats, including forests, cities, farmlands, and open desert. Makes its nest in trees, caves, or on the ground, with a normal clutch resulting in two eggs.

Local Sites
Common throughout the year in California.

FIELD NOTES Among the most common myths surrounding owls are: their inactivity during the day, their inability to see during the day, and their increased ability to see at night. Actually, owls hunt during the day as well as at night, and their nighttime hunts are usually governed more by hearing than by sight.

Year-round | Adult

WESTERN SCREECH-OWL

Megascops kennicottii L 8½" (22 cm)

FIELD MARKS

Gray to brown overall; streaked plumage

Yellow eyes

Visible ear tufts

Dark bill

Large white spots on wings

Behavior

Tends to roost next to tree trunks, where its cryptic coloration blends with the bark's color and pattern. Nocturnal and a sit-and-wait predator, this small owl feeds heavily on insects, sometimes gleaning them from foliage, or hawking them from the air like a flycatcher. When hunting, it will perch on an outer branch for a better view of its territory. Also feeds on small mammals, birds, and even fish. A cavity nester. Habitually decapitates prey before feeding it to chicks.

Habitat

Open woodlands, streamside groves, deserts, suburban areas, and parks. Prefers low-altitude riparian habitats and deciduous forests. Has adapted to human activity; readily roosts and nests in wooded suburban areas.

Local Sites

Common year-round in the state, favoring low-elevation parks, forests, water, and deciduous trees.

FIELD NOTES "Owling," or looking for owls at night, is challenging and rewarding. Scout an area during the day. Streaks of white-wash on a tree trunk and pellet casts at the base of a tree indicate a roost site. If the owl is absent during the day, return at night when the owl may be using the site as a hunting roost.

Year-round | Adult

BURROWING OWL

Athene cunicularia L 9½" (24 cm)

FIELD MARKS

Long legs; short tail

Large, yellow eyes

White streaking on head; white chin and throat

Brown upperparts with white spotting; pale underparts

Behavior

Forages primarily at night, dawn, and dusk on insects and small mammals, such as mice. Flight low and undulating; can hover like a kestrel. Regularly perches on the ground during the day next to its burrow. Nests in single pairs or small colonies. Call is a series of soft *coo-cooo* notes or a chattering series of *chack* notes. When disturbed in its nest, the Burrowing Owl often gives an alarm call that imitates a rattlesnake.

Habitat

Open grasslands and prairies. Often associated with prairie-dog towns. Has adapted to man-made environments such as golf courses and airports.

Local Sites

While the Burrowing Owl breeds in the middle to eastern part of the state, it lives year-round along the southern coast.

FIELD NOTES Like all owls, Burrowing Owls have feet that are zygodactyl, meaning the outer toe can rotate or pivot back and forth. By this spreading of the toes, these birds form a radially symmetrical web with their feet, an adaptation that helps them snare their prey as it runs to escape.

Year-round | Adult female *sennetti*

COMMON NIGHTHAWK

Chordeiles minor L 9½" (24 cm)

FIELD MARKS

Long, pointed wings with pale spotting; tail slightly forked

Bold white bar across primaries; white tail band in males; dark, mottled back

Underparts whitish, with bold dusky bars; darker in males

Behavior
The Common Nighthawk's streamlined body allows for agile aerial displays when feeding at dusk. Hunts in flight, snaring insects. Capable of dropping lower jaw to create an opening wide enough to scoop in large moths. Roosts on the ground, scraping a shallow depression, or on branches, posts, and roofs. Call is a nasal *peent*. Male's white throat may play a role in mating rituals. Throat is pale buff in females.

Habitat
Seen in woodlands and shrubby areas, as well as in towns and even some cities. May often be seen feeding near bright city lights, to which insects are drawn.

Local Sites
Spends breeding seasons in central California and migrates as far south as Argentina for the winter. Observe it at dusk in Bodie State Historic Park or Yosemite National Park.

FIELD NOTES The Lesser Nighthawk, *Chordeiles acutipennis* (inset), can be distinguished from the Common Nighthawk by shorter, more rounded wings and a white bar closer to the wingtip that does not fully cross the primaries. More common in dry open country, scrubland, and desert.

Year-round | Adult

WHITE-THROATED SWIFT

SWIFTS

Aeronautes saxatalis L 6½" (17 cm)

FIELD MARKS

White chin, breast, and center belly

White oval patch on flanks

Black upperparts

Long, forked tail, looks pointed when not spread

Behavior

Fast-flying bird with fidgety flight patterns. Its long wings bend closer to the body than those of similar swallows. Because of legs and feet poorly adapted to the ground, swifts do not perch during the day. They spend the time in flight, foraging for insects and ballooning spiders, drinking water, bathing, and gathering nest-building materials. Their magnificent roosts are used over and over again. White-throated Swift roosts may harbor up to 500 birds. Roosts are for nonbreeding birds to gather warmth on cold days, which allows them to preserve fat or gain weight for upcoming migration. Call is a *scree.*

Habitat

Common in mountains, canyons, and cliffs; nests in caves and behind waterfalls.

Local Sites

Winters through the south in Mojave Desert area. Breeding range through Yosemite and Mono Lake area.

FIELD NOTES Pairs copulate in air, locking together and spiraling downward for several hundred feet. These swifts have been reported to outfly Peregrine Falcons in stoops approaching 200 mph, which would make them the fastest North American bird.

Year-round | Adult male

BLACK-CHINNED HUMMINGBIRD

Archilochus alexandri L 3¾" (10 cm)

FIELD MARKS

Male shows black throat with violet lower border, white collar

Female shows whitish throat, sometimes streaked greenish

Metallic green above, white below

Dusky-green sides and flanks

Behavior

Hovers to forage nectar and pollen from flowers with its long bill. May leave a perch to catch small flying insects. Twitches tail while hovering, and can fly backward. Like many hummingbirds, often bathes in water or by hovering against wet foliage. Courtship flight consists of male flying in pendulum pattern, vibrating its wings to make a buzzing sound as it passes a perched female on the downslope. Call is a soft *tchew*. Chase note combines high squeals and *tchew*s.

Habitat

Common in lowlands and low mountains. Prefers hot, dry areas. Nests in forks of small branches, generally not far off the ground.

Local Sites

Frequents the southern coastal lowlands, the Central and San Joaquin Valleys, and the Colorado River in summer. Big Morongo Canyon Preserve is a good spot.

FIELD NOTES Beginning in the 1980s, reports of "western" hummingbirds east of their normal range greatly increased. Whether a result of increased observer awareness, more feeders, or simple expansion of range, the Black-chinned Hummingbird now visits the southeastern United States annually in the winter.

Year-round | Adult female

ANNA'S HUMMINGBIRD

Calypte anna L 4" (10 cm)

FIELD MARKS

Deep rose-red head, throat, and sides of neck in male

Female shows white throat speckled with red; green crown and nape

Grayish underparts washed with varying amounts of green

Behavior

Hovers to gather nectar, catches flying insects, and is known to pluck spiders from their webs. May bathe by hovering against foliage covered by early morning dew. Common call note is a sharp *chick;* chase call a rapid, dry rattling; male's song a jumble of high squeaks and raspy notes, developed over time and incorporating various phrases and elements learned from neighbors.

Habitat

Abundant in coastal lowlands, suburban settings, mountains, and deserts, especially in winter. Essentially nonmigratory, the range of this adaptable bird is expanding northward.

Local Sites

Can be spotted on the Bayside Trail of Cabrillo National Monument, southwest of San Diego, and at nearby Lake Hodges.

FIELD NOTES The deep violet gorget of the male Costa's Hummingbird, *Calypte costae* (inset), extends onto the crown and down the sides of the neck, much like the Anna's. This species, though, is more common in the desert washes and dry chaparral of southern California.

Year-round | Adult male

RUFOUS HUMMINGBIRD

Selasphorus rufus L 3¾" (10 cm)

FIELD MARKS

Male rufous above, rufous wash
below; orange-red gorget

Female has green upperparts and
white, speckled throat

Both show white breast patch
extending down center of belly

Behavior

Makes one of the longest migrations relative to body
size of any bird, needing frequent and expedient
refueling. Highly aggressive temperament; drives
away competitors up to three times its size, including
blackbirds, thrushes, even chipmunks. Highly intoler-
ant of other birds at feeders. Courtship flight consists
of male ascending with back to female, then diving and
turning on its whistling wings with orange-red gorget
showing. Calls include a sibilant *chip*, often given in a
series, and a chase note of *zeee-chuppity-chup*.

Habitat

Found in Pacific Northwest in the summer, wherever
suitable nectar can be found. Nests in limbs of trees.

Local Sites

The Rufous's summer range barely touches California
in the north. Best bet is to fill a feeder with sugar water
and offer a stop-off during their long migration.

FIELD NOTES This hummingbird is especially attracted to the
color red, preferring such flowers as the columbine and the tiger
lily for their nectar. It will even hover to investigate a red T-shirt
or magazine cover.

Year-round | Adult male

ALLEN'S HUMMINGBIRD

Selasphorus sasin L 3¾" (10 cm)

FIELD MARKS

Male has full orange-red gorget

White patch below throat extends
as a line onto center of belly

Green crown and back

Rufous sides, flanks, belly, rump,
and tail

Behavior
A solitary forager, it hovers to sip flower nectar with its
needlelike bill. May also catch flying insects or pluck
them from spiderwebs. Drinks sap from drill holes as
well. An aggressive defender of its territory, known to
attack and evict even hawks from nesting area. Courtship flight consists of steep dive followed by slight
ascent and hovering position with gorget showing.

Habitat
Very adaptable, found in suburban settings as well
as chaparral and thickets in more arid landscapes.
Summers along the coast of California, but heads
farther south in early fall.

Local Sites
Look for one subspecies of the Allen's year-round
on Santa Rosa, Santa Cruz, Santa Catalina, and San
Clemente Islands, and in Los Angeles County. The
other subspecies is found along the coast from Santa
Barbara County north in the summer.

FIELD NOTES The female and immature Allen's Hummingbirds are
virtually identical in the field to the Rufous Hummingbird. Only
the sharpest eyes can tell that the Rufous's tail feathers are
slightly wider. The adult male Allen's Hummingbird is easily distinguished by its solid green crown and back.

Year-round | Adult male

BELTED KINGFISHER

Ceryle alcyon L 13" (33 cm)

FIELD MARKS
Blue-gray head with large,
shaggy crest

Blue-gray upperparts and breast
band; white underparts and collar

Long, heavy, black bill

Chestnut sides, belly band in female

Behavior
Generally solitary and vocal, dives for fish from a
waterside perch or after hovering above to line up on
its target. Will also forage for frogs, insects, amphibians, and small reptiles. Call is a loud, dry rattle, often
given when alarmed, to demonstrate territory, or while
in flight.

Habitat
Common and conspicuous along rivers, ponds, lakes,
and estuaries. Prefers areas that are partially wooded.

Local Sites
Resides year-round throughout much of California,
and winters in southern regions. Look for these compact fish-eaters around the Sacramento and Colusa
National Wildlife Refuges.

FIELD NOTES Pairs are monogamous
and nest in burrows they dig three or
more feet into vertical earthen banks
near watery habitats. Both sexes carry
out the work in building the nest, and they also share parenting
duties for their clutches of three to eight. Mated pairs renew their
relationship with each breeding season, using courtship rituals
such as dramatic display flights, the feeding of the female by the
male, and vocalizations.

Year-round | Adult female

ACORN WOODPECKER

Melanerpes formicivorus L 9" (23 cm)

FIELD MARKS

Red cap

Distinct whitish eye

Black chin, yellowish throat; white cheeks and forehead

Female has smaller bill and less red on crown

Behavior

A sociable bird, the Acorn Woodpecker can be found in a small, noisy colony, drilling small holes into a tree trunk and pounding a nut into each hole for a winter supply. Will aggressively defend its store and nests from squirrels and other birds. Colony will use the same "granary tree" year after year. The bird can be seen in summer, foraging on trunks for insects or giving chase to them. Drinks from sap holes and feeders. Call is a repeated *waka waka waka*.

Habitat

Common in oak woods and in pine forests where oak trees are abundant. Nests communally in holes drilled into stumps or dead trees. Several adults share in duties of incubating and feeding young.

Local Sites

Look in the forests of the coastal ranges, especially at Ano Nuevo.

FIELD NOTES Males of the related Gila Wood-pecker, *Melanerpes uropygialis* (inset), share with the Acorn Woodpecker a red cap, but are easily distinguished by the black-and-white barred back. Look for them along the Colorado River.

Year-round | Adult male

WHITE-HEADED WOODPECKER

Picoides albolarvatus L 9¼" (24 cm)

FIELD MARKS
White head and throat
Male shows red occipital patch
Black postocular stripe
Black body
Bold white wing patches

Behavior

Feeds primarily on seeds, which it can extract directly from unopened pinecones, while maintaining a distance with its legs so that its feathers do not take on sap. Also pries away loose bark in search of insects, spiders, and larvae. Will drill horizontal rows of sap wells on tree bark. Calls include a sharp *pee-dink* or *pee-dee-dink* and a rattle that descends at the end, given in flight or at rest.

Habitat

Resides in coniferous mountain forests, especially ponderosa and sugar pine. Casual at lower altitudes in winter. Nests in holes bored into stumps or trees throughout its range.

Local Sites

Look for the White-headed perching, sometimes sideways or even upside down, on the trunks of pines in Klamath National Forest, Modoc National Forest, Stanislaus National Forest, or Angeles National Forest.

FIELD NOTES Male and female White-headed Woodpeckers will partition their foraging into microhabitats, with the females feeding down low on ponderosa pines and incense cedars, and the males feeding higher up on the same trees and on Coulter pines.

Year-round | Adult male "Yellow-shafted"

NORTHERN FLICKER

Colaptes auratus L 12½" (32 cm)

FIELD MARKS

Brown, barred back; cream underparts with black spotting; black crescent bib

Brown crown and gray face

Red crescent on nape ("Yellow-shafted"); or red moustachial stripe ("Red-shafted")

Behavior

Feeds mostly on the ground, primarily on ants, but is a cavity-nesting bird that will drill into wooden surfaces above ground, including utility poles and houses. Call is a long, loud series of *wick-er, wick-er* on the breeding ground, or a single, loud *klee-yer* year-round.

Habitat

Prefers open woodlands and suburban areas with sizeable living and dead trees. As insectivores, they are partially migratory, and move southward in the winter in pursuit of food.

Local Sites

A year-round resident of most of the state, will winter in the extreme southeastern part of California. Look for the Northern Flicker around Mono Lake Country Park and areas northward.

FIELD NOTES Two distinct groups make up the Northern Flicker species. The "Red-shafted Flicker" occurs mainly in the western United States, and the other, the "Yellow-shafted Flicker" (image opposite), does appear in the West in the fall and winter, although it is more commonly seen in the eastern and northern United States. Their habits and habitats are similar.

Year-round | Adult *daggetti*

RED-BREASTED SAPSUCKER

Sphyrapicus ruber L 8½" (22 cm)

FIELD MARKS

Red head, nape, and breast

Black back spotted with white or yellow

Yellow to pale-yellow wash on belly

Large white wing patch in flight

Behavior

Drills even rows of holes in trees and strips bark to produce sap flow, then feeds on sap, insects it attracts, and berries. Often silent, it can emit a plaintive *mew* call, but its biggest sound comes from the staccato pounding of its bill on wood, made possible by the well-adapted bone and muscle structure of its head, which can absorb a tremendous amount of shock.

Habitat

Common in coniferous or mixed forests in coastal Pacific ranges. Northern subspecies *ruber* nests in living deciduous trees at low elevations; southern subspecies *daggetti*, with white spots on back and a white moustachial stripe, nests in conifers, alders, or willows near water. Most migrate south or move to lower elevations in winter.

Local Sites

Winters in the Central and San Joaquin Valleys. The *daggetti* subspecies lives at higher elevations year-round.

FIELD NOTES One of the few woodpecker species with identical plumage in both the male and female. The birds breed in small, loose colonies, and their relationship is believed to be monogamous. Young are fed by the male.

Year-round | Adult

NUTTALL'S WOODPECKER

Picoides nuttallii L 7½" (19 cm)

FIELD MARKS

Black forecrown, ear patches

Red occipital patch in male

White chin, throat, and underparts

Alternating black-and-white stripe down center of back

Black spots on sides

Behavior

Often alights upside down on underside of branch. Like all woodpeckers, when it climbs up tree bark, it hops upward with two feet together, propelled by its tail. Forages singly or in pairs, seeking insects in the bark of oak trees, usually by probing crevices and chipping away dead bark instead of drilling. Call is a rattled *prrrt*, lower in pitch than the *pik* of its close relative, the Ladder-backed. Also gives a series of loud, spaced, descending notes. Has a long drum.

Habitat

Seen in chaparral mixed with scrub oak, wooded canyons, and streamside trees. Nests in tree cavities.

Local Sites

Year-round on California coast. Visible around Morro Rock at Morro Bay, near San Luis Obispo, and at Angeles National Forest in the San Gabriel Mountains north of Los Angeles.

FIELD NOTES When foraging, Nuttall's females prefer smaller branches than males do, and they forage higher. The amount of time male and female spend probing, gleaning, or tapping also differs. Such division of labor is thought to win a pair a wider variety of prey, a benefit in feeding young in breeding season.

Year-round | Adult

DOWNY WOODPECKER

Picoides pubescens L 6¾" (17 cm)

FIELD MARKS

White belly, back, outer tail feathers

Black, stubby bill

Black malar stripe, cap, ear patch, nape, shoulders, central tail feathers

Red occipital patch in male

Behavior
The smallest woodpecker in North America, forages mainly on insects, larvae, and eggs. Will also eat seeds, and readily visits backyard feeders for sunflower seeds and suet. Also known to consume poison-ivy berries. Call is a high-pitched but soft *pik*. Note the dull spots or bars on the white outer tailfeathers.

Habitat
Common in suburbs, parks, and orchards, as well as forests and woodlands.

Local Sites
A year-round resident of the northern three-quarters of the state, although not found in the valley north of Sacramento. These unwary insectivores are usually very easily spotted throughout their range.

FIELD NOTES The larger Hairy Woodpecker, *Picoides villosus*, 9¼" (24 cm) in length, is similarly marked, but has a bill as long as the depth of its head and sports white outer tail feathers that are unmarked. Young males of this species show spots of white on their foreheads, and their crowns are streaked with red or orange.

Nonbreeding | Adult

PACIFIC-SLOPE FLYCATCHER

Empidonax difficilis L 5½" (14 cm)

FIELD MARKS

Large olive head

Broad bill with black upper, orange lower mandibles

Pale teardrop eye ring, expanded behind eye, broken above

Brown-green above, yellow below

Behavior

Flycatchers are solitary and active birds, noted for perching in the upright position and often flicking wings and tail. With broad, hook-tipped bill, a Pacific Flycatcher snatches flying insects from its shaded perch and gleans insects from foliage. Bristles at the base of the bill are thought to inform the bird of movement of prey. Leaves one perch to fly after food, then returns to a new perch. Builds cup-shaped nests.

Habitat

Common in moist woodlands, coniferous forests, and in California's shady canyons. Prefers lowlands that skirt mountain areas.

Local Sites

Breeds along the California coast; winters in western Mexico lowlands. Visible along forest trails of Point Reyes National Seashore, in Montana de Oro State Park, and at the Santa Barbara Botanical Gardens.

FIELD NOTES Worldwide, Birdlife International classifies 25 species of flycatcher as threatened, and 23 as near threatened. The most threatened is the southwestern subspecies of Willow Flycatcher. It lives in non-native tamarisk trees—a dilemma for conservationists, who would otherwise want to discourage growth of the invasive alien plant.

Year-round | Adult

WESTERN WOOD-PEWEE

Contopus sordidulus L 6¼" (16 cm)

FIELD MARKS

Dark grayish brown overall; pale underparts

Broad, flat bill; yellow-orange at base of lower mandible

Bristly whiskers

Two thin white wing bars

Behavior

Solitary and often hidden in trees. As it perches, it looks actively about, without flicking tail or wings. When prey is spotted, it darts out to catch a variety of flies, spiders, butterflies, wasps, ants, and dragonflies. Returns to the same perch. Bristly whiskers help it locate prey. Calls include a harsh, slightly descending *peeer,* and clear whistles suggestive of the Eastern Wood-Pewee's *pee-yer.* Song is heard chiefly on breeding grounds and has three-note *tswee-tee-teet* phrases mixed with the *peeer* note.

Habitat

Common in open woodlands, but not found in the United States during winter.

Local Sites

Breeds throughout California; winters exclusively in South America.

FIELD NOTES At 7½" (19 cm), the larger Olive-sided Flycatcher, *Contopus cooperi* (inset), shows a streaked vest and a white central breast. It shares essentially the same range with the Western Wood-Pewee, but it can still be seen in winter along the coastal slope of southern California, when the Wood-Pewee has gone south.

Year-round | Adult

BLACK PHOEBE

Sayornis nigricans L 6½" (17 cm)

FIELD MARKS
Black head, breast, upperparts

Straight black bill with slight hook
at tip

White belly and undertail coverts

Behavior
Often seen perching upright on a low, shaded branch,
pumping its tail in a distinctive downward movement.
Waits to spot a flying insect, then goes after it. Frequently returns to a different perch. Has been seen
to take insects and even small fish from the water's
surface. Regurgitates indigestible insect parts in the
form of pellets. Song is a rising *pee-wee* followed by
a descending *pee-wee*. Calls include a loud *tseee* and
a sharper *tsip*, slightly more plaintive than the Eastern
Phoebe's call. Often builds nests in and on man-
made structures.

Habitat
Common in woodlands, suburbs and parks, coastal
sage scrub, and grasslands. Prefers to nest near water.

Local Sites
Find phoebes along the state's coastline, especially in
Coastal Cove State Park and, in the desert, in the lush
oasis of Big Morongo State Preserve.

FIELD NOTES The Black Phoebe and its relatives are thought to
be monogamous, though on rare occasion a male may pair with
two females. In some species, such as the Eastern Phoebe, a
male other than the male attending the nest may father one or
more of the offspring.

Nonbreeding | Adult

WESTERN KINGBIRD

Tyrannus verticalis L 8¾" (22 cm)

FIELD MARKS

Ashy-gray head, neck, and breast

Back tinged with olive

Dark wings contrast with paler back

Lemon-yellow belly

Behavior

Feeding almost exclusively on flying insects, leaves its perch to snatch prey in midair, often returning to the perch to eat. Eats a variety, including flies, spiders, cicadas, grasshoppers, butterflies, and dragonflies. Perches horizontally instead of upright. Courtship display involves aerial flight. Most kingbirds build cup-shaped nests near the end of a horizontal tree branch, lining them with weeds, moss, and feathers. Common and gregarious, nesting pairs regularly share the same tree. Kingbirds have a raspy call when feeding or defending territory—a sharp *whit*.

Habitat

Common in dry, open country. Has also adapted to urban areas. Often perches on fence posts and telephone lines.

Local Sites

Breeds throughout most of California; seen in the desert oasis of Morongo Canyon Preserve.

FIELD NOTES The related Eastern Kingbird actively defends its nests and territories, and will drive off invaders the size of a Red-tailed Hawk. Orchard Orioles are seen to nest nearby, perhaps for safety, due to the kingbird's tenacious defense of its nest area.

Year-round | Adult *macrolopha*

STELLER'S JAY

Cyanocitta stelleri L 11½" (29 cm)

FIELD MARKS

Black head, crest, and bill with
bristles covering nostrils

Dark gray back, neck, and breast

Purplish blue upperparts;
smoky-blue underparts

Narrow black bars on wings, tail

Behavior

Bold and aggressive, the only crested jay in the West.
Often seen in large flocks and family groups, feeding
from the treetops to the ground. Often scavenges in
campgrounds and picnic areas. Powerful bill efficiently
handles a varied diet. Forages during warm months on
insects, frogs, carrion, young birds, and eggs. Winter
diet is mainly acorns and seeds. Hides food for later
consumption. Highly social, jays will stand sentry,
ready to mob predators, while others in the flock
forage. Large numbers roost together to share heat at
night. Calls include a series of *shack* or *shooka* notes.

Habitat

Common in pine-oak woods and coniferous forests.

Local Sites

Winter visitor to lower elevations in California, is seen
on Mount Pinos, in Los Padres National Forest, and in
the San Gabriel Mountains of Angeles National Forest.

FIELD NOTES All jays are known as hoarders of food. A relative of
the Steller, the Gray Jay, *Perisoreus canadensis,* uses its sticky
saliva to insert and store food into crevices and under tree bark.
Such caching helps with plant dispersal, since some forgotten or
uneaten seeds may germinate and help revitalize forests.

Year-round | Adult *californica*

WESTERN SCRUB-JAY

Apheloma californica L 11" (28 cm)

FIELD MARKS
Dark blue upperparts; whitish to buff underparts

White eyebrow; dark eye patch

Whitish, streaked throat

Variable bluish band on chest

Undertail coverts may be bluish

Behavior
Seen in pairs and small flocks, foraging on ground and in trees for insects, fruit, seeds, grain, eggs, baby birds, and small reptiles and mammals. Jays' strong legs allow for steady ground foraging. Strong, stout bills allow a wide-ranging diet. Jays often help the flock by standing sentry during foraging; together they mob would-be predators. Usually roost together at night for warmth. Calls include a raspy *shreep,* often in a short series.

Habitat
Tame and widespread, often seen in urban settings perched in the open in trees and shrubs.

Local Sites
Found year-round throughout the state, often in Santa Barbara Botanic Garden and the sagebrush scrub of the South Tufa area near Mono Lake.

FIELD NOTES With rich blue undertail coverts, the Island Scrub-Jay, *Apheloma insularis* (inset), is larger and more colorful than its relatives, the Western and Florida species. Until recently, all were considered one species. Now they are three. The Island is more wary than the other jays. Its range is restricted to Santa Cruz Island.

Year-round | Adult

ISLAND SCRUB-JAY

Aphalocoma coerulescens L 11" (28cm)

FIELD MARKS

Distinct white eyebrow

Large bill

Long tail with rich blue undertail coverts

Deep blue above with contrasting brown patch; blue breast band

Behavior

More wary than other jays, which are noted for their gregarious nature. Forages on its strong legs for insects, fruit, seeds, acorns, grain, eggs, even small mammals. Uses its strong, stout bill for eating its varied diet. Often seen perching low in the shade of a scrub oak, probably guarding its territory. Island Scrub-Jays have a cooperative breeding system: Fledged young remain in territory where they hatched and help rear new broods of nestlings, so it takes several years for a young bird to acquire its own nesting territory. Call is identical to the Western Scrub-Jay's: a raspy *shreep* in a short series.

Habitat

On Santa Cruz Island, its only home, it frequents scrub oak and ironwood trees. Also eucalyptus and other local plants near water.

Local Sites

Restricted to Santa Cruz Island, in California's Channel Islands, where it is the only scrub-jay.

FIELD NOTES Although the Island Scrub-Jay is common on Santa Cruz, there is concern for the future of the species. Whenever a small population is isolated, weather extremes, epidemics, or human development can produce a catastrophic decline.

Year-round | Adult

BLACK-BILLED MAGPIE

Pica hudsonia L 19" (48 cm)

FIELD MARKS

Black upperparts, breast, and undertail coverts

Black bill

White sides and belly

White wing patches

Behavior

Gregarious and noisy, Black-billed Magpies forage on the ground in family flocks of up to a dozen birds, feeding on insects and carrion. They are hoarders of food for later consumption and also of shiny nonfood items such as aluminum foil, glass shards, and even forks. May feed on the eggs of other birds. Typical calls include whining *mag* and a series of loud, harsh *chuck* notes. Pair bonds among magpies are probably for life.

Habitat

Common inhabitant of open woodlands, thickets, rangelands, and foothills, especially along watercourses in northeastern California.

Local Sites

Year-round range is in northeastern California, from Tule Lake National Wildlife Reserve in the north to Yosemite National Park and Mono Lake mid-state. Winters along the Pacific Coast.

FIELD NOTES The Black-billed's relative, the Yellow-billed Magpie, *Pica nuttalli* (inset), is distinguished by a yellow bill and a yellow skin patch near eye. It roosts in closer colonies than do Black-billeds.

Year-round | Adult

AMERICAN CROW

Corvus brachyrhynchos L 17½" (45 cm)

FIELD MARKS
Long, heavy, black bill
Black, iridescent plumage overall
Fan-shaped tail
Brown eyes
Readily identified by familiar call

Behavior
Omnivorous. Often forages in flocks, feeding on insects, garbage, grain, mice, eggs, and baby birds. Crows take turns on sentry duty, perching on guard while a flock feeds, and are regularly seen noisily mobbing large predators like eagles, hawks, and Great Horned Owls. Bills are impressive, but not able to tear through hides and open carcasses, so crows instead wait for another predator—or automobile—to open up a carcass for dining. Most readily identified by its familiar call, *caw caw*.

Habitat
Among the most widely distributed and familiar birds in North America. Lives in a variety of habitats.

Local Sites
Common throughout its range. Readily viewed in the vicinity of landfills and agricultural operations.

FIELD NOTES At 24" (61 cm), the Common Raven, *Corvus corax* (inset), is larger than the American Crow, and is readily identifiable by its guttural croaking call and its wedge-shaped tail, seen in flight.

Year-round | Adult female *alpestris*

HORNED LARK

Eremophila alpestris L 6¾"-7¾" (17 cm-20 cm)

White forehead bordered by black band, which ends in hornlike tufts

Black cheek stripes; black bill

Pale yellow to white throat and underparts; brown upperparts

Sandy wash on sides and flanks

Behavior

Forages on ground, favoring open agricultural fields with sparse vegetation. Feeds mainly on seeds, grain, and some insects. Seldom alights on trees or bushes. On the ground, the Horned Lark walks rather than hops. Song is a weak twittering; calls include a high *tsee-ee* or *tsee-titi*. Outside breeding season, the birds form large flocks that may number into the hundreds. They use their bills and feet with long hindclaws to create shallow depressions where they roost and nest. Females build the nest and incubate the clutch; both sexes feed the young.

Habitat

Prefers dirt fields, gravel ridges, and shores.

Local Sites

See them year-round throughout California, except in the extreme northwest or eastern mountain region. Places include the semidesert Carrizo Plain Natural Area in southern California, east of San Luis Obispo.

FIELD NOTES The male engages in a spectacular display flight, ascending several hundred feet into the air while singing, then plummeting headfirst toward the ground, flaring wings at the last second.

Breeding | Adult

Tachycineta bicolor L 5¾" (15 cm)

FIELD MARKS

Dark, glossy, greenish blue above; white below

White cheek patch does not extend above eye

Slightly notched tail

Behavior

Often seen in huge flocks, especially during migration and in winter. Forages on insects in flight and changes to a diet of berries or plant buds during colder months, when insects are less abundant. Plumage changes to a more greenish hue in fall. Juvenile sports a gray-brown color above.

Habitat

Common to wooded habitats near water, or where dead trees provide nest holes. Also lives in man-made birdhouses.

Local Sites

A migratory bird, the Tree Swallow is the species most often seen in extreme southern California over the winter. It migrates through northern California in spring and fall, and lives year-round in the central part of the state. Other swallow species tend to winter further south.

FIELD NOTES The Violet-Green Swallow, *Tachycineta thalassina* (inset), can be distinguished from the Tree Swallow by the white cheek patch that hooks above the eye.

Year-round | Adult male

BARN SWALLOW

Hirundo rustica L 6¾" (17 cm)

FIELD MARKS

Long, deeply forked tail

Reddish brown throat

Iridescent blue-black upperparts
and breast band

Cinnamon or buff underparts

Behavior

An exuberant flyer, it is often seen in small flocks
skimming low over the surface of a field or pond,
taking insects in midair. Will follow tractors and lawn
mowers to feed on flushed insects. Nests in pairs or
small colonies.

Habitat

Frequents open farms and fields, especially near water.
Has adapted to humans to the extent that it now nests
almost exclusively in structures such as barns, bridges,
culverts, and garages. Nest is bowl-shaped, made of
mud, and lined with grass and feathers.

Local Sites

Can be seen during migration throughout California,
and breeds in all but the extreme southeast portion of
the state. In the fall, it departs on a lengthy flight to
its wintering grounds in Central and
South America.

FIELD NOTES The Barn Swallow shares essentially the same range with the Cliff Swallow,
Petrochelidon pyrrhonota (inset)—distinguished
by its squarish tail, buffy rump, and whitish forehead—and the more plainly plumaged Northern Rough-
winged Swallow, *Stelgidopteryx serripennis*, with its brown
upperparts and whitish underparts.

Year-round | Adult *affabilis*

OAK TITMOUSE

Baeolophus inornatus L 5" (13 cm)

FIELD MARKS
Short crest
Grayish brown upperparts
Paler gray face and underparts
Short, stout bill
Light gray legs and feet

Behavior
Feeds on seeds, acorns, and insects that it gleans from foliage and occasionally catches on the wing. Titmice avoid flying long distances at any one time and prefer to take short flights from tree to tree. Call is a hoarse *tschick-a-dee*, and song is a variable, repeated series of syllables made up of whistled notes, alternating high and low.

Habitat
Common in warm, dry oak woodlands.

Local Sites
Year-round range extends from Baja California northward along the coast, then into central California north to Washington. See titmice in Santa Barbara, on Mount Pinos in Los Padres National Forest, and in the San Gabriel Mountains of Angeles National Forest.

FIELD NOTES The Juniper Titmouse, *Baeolophus ridgwayi* (inset), was until recently considered the same species as the Oak Titmouse. This larger, paler gray titmouse is found mainly in the pinion-juniper woodlands of the eastern California border.

Year-round | Adult *gambeli*

MOUNTAIN CHICKADEE

Poecile gambeli L 5¼" (13 cm)

FIELD MARKS

Black cap, bib, and eye stripe

Distinctive white eyebrow

Grayish upperparts; pale gray underparts

Sometimes tinged with buff on back, sides, and flanks

Behavior

Seen in pairs or small groups, including mixed-species feeding flocks, after breeding season. Forages for insects, spiders, and conifer seeds by gleaning bark, branches, and foliage, often hanging upside down to reach undersides of plants. Chickadees are primarily nonmigratory, but move downslope in winter for warmer temperatures and more available forage.

Habitat

Prefers coniferous and mixed woodlands in mountainous regions, sometimes descending into lower elevations in the winter.

Local Sites

Year-round resident of hilly or mountainous portions of eastern California. Range extends southward into interior of the state toward Baja. Irregular in coastline locations in winter.

FIELD NOTES With bright white cheeks and chestnut plumage, the Chestnut-backed Chickadee, *Poecile rufescens* (inset), inhabits coniferous forests and deciduous woodlands along the California coast, from San Francisco south. Shows less chestnut coloring than the northern birds.

Year-round | Adult male

BUSHTIT

Psaltriparus minimus L 4½" (12 cm)

FIELD MARKS

Gray above, paler below

Coastal birds have brown crown

Interior birds show brown ear patch and gray cap

Noticeably long tail

Behavior

Seen traveling and foraging in noisy flocks of 5 to 30 or more birds, gleaning insects, eggs, and larvae from shrubs and trees. So inconspicuous, it might not be observed at all until a group streams from a foraging site in a long, continuous, undulating file. Its nest is an elaborate, gourd-shaped hanging structure, often fastened in place with spiderwebs. Mistletoe is its nest site of choice, with bottom of sack oriented to receive morning sun.

Habitat

Common in woodlands, parks, chaparral, and gardens.

Local Sites

Is seen year-round throughout coastal and extreme western parts of the state, but not in southeastern California.

FIELD NOTES A relative, the long-tailed, chickadee-like Wrentit, *Chamaea fasciata* (inset), varies from reddish brown in the north to grayer in the south. The Verdin, *Auriparus flaviceps*, a gray bird with yellow head and chestnut shoulder patches, is a chickadee-style feeder that lives in the southern desert.

Year-round | Adult *carolinensis*

WHITE-BREASTED NUTHATCH

Sitta carolinensis L 5¾" (15 cm)

FIELD MARKS

Black cap

All-white face and breast

Thin, black bill, tip slightly upturned

Blue-gray upperparts

Rust below to variable extents

Behavior
An active, nimble feeder. Often spirals around a tree trunk, head down, foraging for insects in bark crevices. Readily visits backyard feeders, preferring sunflower seeds. Typical song is a rapid series of nasal whistles on one pitch.

Habitat
The White-breasted Nuthatch prefers wooded areas full of oak and conifers. These birds make their homes in abandoned woodpecker holes or natural cavities in decaying trees.

Local Sites
Common year-round throughout most of the state, with the exception of extreme south-eastern California.

FIELD NOTES The White-breasted is the largest and most widely distributed nuthatch in North America. The bold, Red-breasted Nuthatch, *Sitta canadensis* (inset), will eat from the hand. It is known to spread pine pitch around its cavity entrance in order to protect its young from predators. The Pygmy Nuthatch, *Sitta pygmaea,* is often seen foraging in loose flocks.

Year-round | Adult

HOUSE WREN

Troglodytes aedon L 4¾" (12 cm)

FIELD MARKS
Faint eyebrow

Thin, slightly decurved bill

Grayish brown upperparts

Pale gray underparts

Fine black barring on wings
and tail

Behavior
Noisy, conspicuous, and relatively tame as it boldly
gleans insects, spiders, and snails from vegetation.
While most species of wren forage low to the ground,
the House Wren will seek food at a variety of levels,
including high in the trees. Sings exuberantly, in a
cascade of bubbling, whistled notes.

Habitat
Highly tolerant of human presence, commonly found
in shrubbery around farms, parks, and urban gardens.

Local Sites
This migratory bird is resident year-round on the
coastline from San Francisco southward. Breeds in the
northern and western portions of the state, and winters
in extreme southern California.

FIELD NOTES Although the House Wren is the smallest wren
species found in North America, it is very competitive when
searching for nest sites and often invades nests of other songbirds, puncturing their eggs and killing their young. The male
may also begin construction at a number of sites before a pre-
ferred location is chosen. Then the mated pair will complete the
nest together, lining the inside with grass and feathers.

Year-round | Adult

WINTER WREN

Troglodytes troglodytes L 4" (10 cm)

FIELD MARKS

Dark brown upperparts with faint
barring

Heavily barred tail, flanks, and
underparts

Rich buff on throat

Short, stubby tail; stocky body

Behavior
Tends to be solitary when not paired for breeding.
An active ground feeder, it constantly bobs and flicks
its tail as it gleans insects and berries from brush and
dense thickets. Song is a melodious series of trills;
call is a *timp-timp*.

Habitat
Secretive inhabitant of dense brush in moist,
coniferous woods, especially along stream banks.

Local Sites
Year-round resident of coastal California, from San
Francisco northward up to the Oregon border, and
across toward the Nevada border. Winter visitor to
locations between San Luis Obispo and Santa Barbara.
Some Winter Wrens migrate into Canada to breed.

FIELD NOTES At 4" long, the Winter Wren is one of the smallest
songbirds in North America. It is the only member of the family
to have spread out from the New World by crossing the Bering
Strait from Alaska long ago. It now appears throughout Asia and
Europe. Its migration is chiefly nocturnal. The eastern varieties of
Winter Wren are lighter in color overall, with more creamy
plumage on the throat.

Year-round | Adult *eremophilus*

BEWICK'S WREN

Thryomanes bewickii L 5¼" (13 cm)

FIELD MARKS
Grayish brown upperparts
Long, white eyebrow
Long, slightly decurved bill
Long tail edged with white spots
Dark gray legs

Behavior
Vocal birds, wrens are usually heard before they are seen. Movement in dense shrubbery may be the first visible sign of them. The Bewick's Wren is often seen in pairs. Feeds mostly on ground but also gleans insects from vegetation. Will add some fruits, berries, and seeds to its diet in the winter. Holds its tail high over its back, often flicking it from side to side. Song is a variable, high, thin buzz and warble. Call includes a flat, hollow *jip*. Male, as among all wrens, defends its breeding territory aggressively.

Habitat
Prefers brushland, hedgerows, stream edges, and open woods.

Local Sites
A year-round resident in most of the state, it visits extreme southeastern portions only in winter.

FIELD NOTES The Bewick's Wren is just one of the renowned singers in the wren family, whose songs attract mates and defend territories. The western Marsh Wren has a varied repertoire of songs—up to 219 of them. Other wrens' songs range from the hoarse tones of the Cactus Wren to the bubbly melody of the House Wren.

Year-round | Adult *sandiegense*

WRENS

CACTUS WREN

Campylorhynchus brunneicapillus L 8½" (22 cm)

FIELD MARKS
Dark crown
Broad, white eyebrow
Streaked back
Heavily barred wings and tail
Breast densely spotted with black

Behavior
Often seen in pairs or small family groups, foraging for
food on the ground or gleaning insects from vegetation. Also feeds on frogs, small lizards, fruit, and nectar.
Its song, heard year-round, is a harsh, low-pitched, and
rapid *cha-cha-cha-cha-cha*. During courtship, a male
wren may chase a visiting female as though she were
an intruder, but the female's call of *chur* announces
that she is interested in him. The male may then hop
stiffly around her and fly to or sing around one of his
nest sites, inviting her to inspect it.

Habitat
Common in cactus country and arid hillsides and
valleys. Fairly bold, the Cactus Wren will offer the
interested birder good, long looks.

Local Sites
Year-round resident of south-central and eastern areas
of California, particularly around the Mojave Desert.

FIELD NOTES North America's largest wren builds its domed
nest in cholla cactus or other thorny plants, where its eggs and
young are protected by the spines of the plant. After the young
birds have fledged, the nests are still maintained by the adults as
roosting sites.

Year-round | Adult male

ROCK WREN

Salpinctes obsoletus L 6" (15 cm)

FIELD MARKS

Gray-brown above, flecked with white

Cinnamon rump

Broad, blackish tail band

Finely streaked breast

Behavior
Frequently bobs its body, especially when alarmed. The Rock Wren's song is a mix of buzzes and trills; its call is a buzzy *tick-ear*.

Habitat
Fairly common in arid and semi-arid regions, it favors sunny talus slopes, scrublands, and dry washes. It usually builds its cup nest in crevices, fissures, or low vegetation.

Local Sites
Common throughout California year-round, except on the extreme northwest coastline and in the central portions. Seen in California's Central Valley during the winter months only. Look for Rock Wrens on a trip into the canyonlands.

FIELD NOTES Rock Wrens are only partially migratory, moving from the norhernmost reaches of their range in the winter months. Their small, stocky build allows them to move about readily in the closed-in, shrubby, rocky habitats they prefer. Additionally, their skulls show some degree of lateral flattening, and their spinal columns are attached farther back on their skulls than those of other wrens. These physiological features allow them to reach more deeply into crevices than most other species with which they compete for food.

Year-round | Adult

MARSH WREN

Cistothorus palustris L 5" (13 cm)

FIELD MARKS
Black cap; bold white eye stripe

Warm brown upperparts with
black-and-white streaking

Rufous sides, flanks, and
undertail coverts

Long, slender bill

Behavior
A chunky bird and secretive marsh denizen that
forages among reeds and grasses for insects, larvae,
snails, and occasionally other birds' eggs. Sings in
liquid notes with slightly harsh tones. The Marsh
Wren's songbook can contain up to 219 different songs.
Call is a sharp *tsuk*, often doubled, when alarmed by an
intruder. Like all wrens, fiercely guards its territory.

Habitat
Common to reedy marshes and cattail swamps.

Local Sites
Like most wrens, the Marsh Wren is often heard before
it is seen. Look for it, though, perched atop tall marsh
reeds in swampy areas like the Arcata Marsh and
Wildlife Sanctuary near Eureka, and throughout much
of the state year-round.

FIELD NOTES The male constructs several football-shaped nests
with side entrances. From those, the female will choose one to
finish for incubation. The male frequently roosts in one of the
dummy nests while tending to multiple mates. This wren also
molts in the spring and the fall, due to feather wear and tear from
living among abrasive plants.

Year-round | Adult

AMERICAN DIPPER

Cinclus mexicanus L 7½" (19 cm)

FIELD MARKS
Sooty-gray overall

Short tail and wings

Straight dark bill

Pink legs and feet

Juvenile has paler, mottled
underparts; pale bill

Behavior
The Dipper is the only songbird that swims. It uses its
wings to propel itself sometimes 20 feet underwater,
then walks on the river bottom to forage into crannies
and under rocks for the larvae of various flies and
mosquitoes. Also eats worms, water bugs, clams, snails,
even small trout. In courtship, male will strut and sing
with wings spread, after which both partners may jump
up and bump breasts. Song is rattling and musical,
loud enough to be heard over river's splash.

Habitat
Found along mountain streams fed by melting snow,
glaciers, and rainfall. Descends to lower elevations in
winter. Nests close to water level on cliffs, midstream
boulders, bridges, or behind waterfalls.

Local Sites
Look for the American Dipper wading in or diving into
the many streams and rivers of the coastal ranges and
of the Cascade-Sierra axis.

FIELD NOTES The American Dipper has the uncanny ability to fly
directly into and out of water. It may sometimes wade in from the
shore and dive from there, but can also dive straight into water
from a low flight.

Year-round | Adult female

GOLDEN-CROWNED KINGLET

Regulus satrapa L 4" (10 cm)

FIELD MARKS

Orange crown patch on male,
bordered in yellow and black;
yellow crown patch on female,
bordered in black

Olive-green upperparts, pale
buff underparts

Broad whitish stripe above eye

Behavior

Hovers on rapidly beating wings before dipping down
to foliage to eat. Also gleans insects, larvae, and seeds
from bark and leaves, reaching into tiny recesses with
its short, straight bill. Flits its wings while hopping on
branches. Song is almost inaudibly high, consisting of
a series of *tsee* notes accelerating into a trill.

Habitat

Common in dense, coniferous woodlands. Nests in
subarctic north and mountainous regions further
south. It is the smallest species able to maintain
normal body temperature in subfreezing conditions.
Nests fairly high in conifer branches, constructing
spherical nest of lichen, moss, bark, and feathers.
Nest is so small that eggs are laid in two layers.

Local Sites

Scan the Klamath, Sierra, or San Bernardino Mountains in summer, and the Sacramento Valley in winter.

FIELD NOTES The male Ruby-crowned Kinglet, *Regulus
calendula*, shows a set of scarlet crown feathers, as distinct from
orange, when it is agitated. It is further distinguished from the
Golden-crowned Kinglet by a white eye ring instead of a supercilium and by its darker, dusky, greenish yellow underparts.

Year-round | Adult male

WESTERN BLUEBIRD

Sialia mexicana L 7" (18 cm)

FIELD MARKS

Chestnut shoulders, upper back

Deep purple-blue upperparts
and throat in male; duller,
brownish gray in female

Chestnut breast, sides, and flanks
in male; chestnut-gray in female

Behavior

Using their large, acute eyes, bluebirds still-hunt from a
perch high above the ground, then swoop down to seize
crickets, grasshoppers, and spiders, which they may
have spotted from as far as 130 feet away. The call note
of the Western Bluebird is a mellow *few,* extended in
brief song to *few few fawee.*

Habitat

Found in woodlands, farmlands, orchards, and deserts
in the winter. Nests in holes in trees or posts as well as
in nest boxes. Frequents mesquite-mistletoe groves.

Local Sites

Lives year-round along the state's west coast and into
the interior. Winters in the valleys around Sacramento.
Breeds in upper northeast and south
toward Lake Tahoe.

FIELD NOTES Contrary to its name, the
Mountain Bluebird, *Sialia currucoides*
(inset), is found primarily in open lowlands and deserts, although it does inhabit rangelands
and meadows above 5,000 feet. It differs from the Western
Bluebird in its blue breast color; in its song, a low, warbled
tru-lee; and in its diet, which contains more insects than
that of any of its relatives.

Year-round | Adult female

AMERICAN ROBIN

Turdus migratorius L 10" (25 cm)

FIELD MARKS

Gray-brown above; darker head and tail

Yellow bill

Brick-red underparts, paler in female

White lower belly

Behavior

Best-known and largest of the thrushes. Very often seen on suburban lawns, hopping about and cocking its head to one side in search of earthworms. The American Robin will also glean butterflies, damselflies, and other flying insects from foliage. Even takes prey in flight. Robins also consume fruit, usually in the fall and winter, making them one of the most successful—and wide-ranging—thrushes.

Habitat

Widespread, the American Robin is seen in the grass on lawns and nesting in shrubs, woodlands, swamps, and parks.

Local Sites

Common in backyards throughout the state. Breadcrumbs in a feeder often get Robins' attention. They are also particularly partial to birdbaths.

FIELD NOTES Cousin to the American Robin, the Hermit Thrush, *Catharus guttatus*, is smaller, with tan-brown upperparts and creamy white underparts with brown spotting. The Varied Thrush, *Ixoreus naevius* (inset), is just slightly smaller than the American Robin and has brown upperparts, reddish orange underparts, and a black or brown breast band.

Year-round | Adult

NORTHERN MOCKINGBIRD

Mimus polyglottos L 10" (25 cm)

FIELD MARK

Gray plumage; dark wings and tail

White wing patches and outer tail feathers, which flash conspicuously in flight

Repeats same phrase several times while singing

Behavior

This popular, widespread mimic learns as many as 200 song types. Males have a spring and fall repertoire. Highly pugnacious, will protect its territory against not only other birds but also dogs, cats, and even humans. Mockingbirds have a varied diet that includes grasshoppers, spiders, snails, and earthworms.

Habitat

Resides in a variety of habitats, including in towns. Feeds close to the ground, often in thickets or in heavy vegetation.

Local Sites

The Northern Mockingbird is a year-round resident throughout much of California. Difficult to locate, listen for its characteristic repeating of song phrases three times before beginning a new one.

FIELD NOTES Though not related, the Loggerhead Shrike, *Lanius ludovicianus* (inset), L 9" (23 cm), looks strikingly similar to the Northern Mockingbird. Note the distinguishing black mask and hooked bill of this falconlike songbird. In flight, the wings and tail are darker and the white wing patches are smaller than in the Northern Mockingbird.

Year-round | Adult

CALIFORNIA THRASHER

Taxostoma redivivum L 12" (31 cm) W 45" (114 cm)

FIELD MARKS

Dark above with pale eyebrow

Dark eyes and cheeks

Pale throat contrasts with
dark breast

Belly and undertail coverts
tawny buff

Behavior

Found primarily on the ground. Forages for insects,
grubs, caterpillars, and spiders by digging and raking
with its long, curved bill. Occasionally eats seed or
fruit. Breeds monogamously per season, and pair
bonds may last for several years. Song is loud and
sustained, with mostly guttural phrases, often repeated
once or twice. A member of family *Mimidae,* which
includes mockingbirds, the California Thrasher is also
known to imitate other species' sounds.

Habitat

Common resident in chaparral-covered foothills of
California and Baja California. Also found in moist
woodlands with thick ground cover, in streamside
thickets, in suburban gardens, and in parks.

Local Sites

Found primarily in the foothills of the Sierras and the
coastal ranges. Among the sage scrub of Cabrillo National
Monument's Bayside Trail is a good spot to look.

FIELD NOTES Though its traditional habitat is being threatened
due to development, agriculture, and golf courses, the California
Thrasher seems to be adapting to suburban sprawl, frequenting
feeders and birdbaths in parks and backyards.

Nonbreeding | Adult

EUROPEAN STARLING

Sturnus vulgaris L 8½" (22 cm)

FIELD MARKS

Iridescent black breeding plumage

Yellow bill, its base blue in male, pink in female

Fall feathers tipped in white and buff, giving speckled appearance; fall bill brownish

Behavior

A highly social and aggressive bird, the European Starling will gorge on a tremendous variety of food, ranging from invertebrates—such as snails, worms, and spiders—to fruits, berries, grains, seeds, and even garbage. Short, square tail is particularly distinguishable during flight. Will imitate the songs of other species and has call notes that include squeaks, warbles, chirps, and twittering. Outside nesting season, usually seen in large flocks.

Habitat

Adaptable, starlings thrive in a variety of habitats, from urban centers to agricultural regions. They nest in cavities, ranging from crevices in urban settings to woodpecker holes and nest boxes.

Local Sites

The European Starling is a widespread year-round resident of California.

FIELD NOTES A Eurasian species introduced to America in the 1890s that has since spread throughout the U.S. and Canada. Abundant, bold, and aggressive, Starlings often compete for and take over nest sites of other birds, including Eastern Bluebirds, Wood Ducks, Red-bellied Woodpeckers, Great Crested Flycatchers, and Purple Martins.

Year-round | Adult male

CEDAR WAXWING

Bombycilla cedrorum L 7¼" (18 cm)

FIELD MARKS

Distinctive sleek crest

Black mask bordered in white

Silky plumage with brownish
chest and upperparts

Yellow terminal tail band

May have red, waxy tips on wings

Behavior

Eats the most fruit of any bird in North America. Up
to 84 percent of diet includes cedar, peppertree, and
hawthorn berries and crabapple fruit. Also consumes
sap, flower petals, and insects. Cedar Waxwings are
gregarious in nature and band together for foraging
and protection. Not strongly territorial, they aggressively defend only their nest, perhaps to guard mate
or nesting material. Flocks containing from a few to
thousands of birds may feed side by side in winter.
Flocks rapidly disperse, startling potential predators.

Habitat

Found in open habitats where berries are available. The
abundance and location of berries influence the Cedar
Waxwing's migration patterns: It moves long distances
only when its food sources run out.

Local Sites

Found throughout the winter in California, wherever
cedars and other fruit-bearing trees are plentiful.

FIELD NOTES Cedar Waxwing mates engage in "courtship
hopping." On a shared perch, male and female take turns hopping
toward one another until they touch bills. The male passes food to
the female. She hops away, returns, and gives it back.

Nonbreeding | Adult female "Myrtle"

YELLOW-RUMPED WARBLER

Dendroica coronata L 5½" (14 cm)

FIELD MARKS

Bright yellow rump

Yellow patch on sides

Yellow crown patch

White wing bars and tail patches

Females and fall males duller than
breeding males

Behavior

Easy to locate and observe darting about the branches
from tree to tree, foraging for insects and spiders in the
spring and summer, for myrtle berries and seeds in
winter. Also drinks tree sap and juice from fallen
oranges. Courtship involves intensive singing. After-
ward nest-building and incubation falls mainly to the
female. Songs of the western subspecies include a slow
warble, rising or falling at end.

Habitat

Abundant in coniferous or mixed woodlands. Nests
discreetly and solitarily on fork or branch of tree.

Local Sites

Look for the Yellow-rumped in southern California in
winter, from the Mojave Desert area west to the San
Gabriel Mountains. Year-round it can be found in the
vicinity of Arcata Wildife Sanctuary in the north, or
around Los Padres National Forest in the south.

FIELD NOTES The eastern subspecies of the Yellow-rumped
Warbler is often referred to as "Myrtle Warbler," distinguishing it
from the western subspecies, "Audubon's Warbler," which has
the same markings, but is darker overall with a yellow instead of
white throat. It also lacks the white eyebrow of the Myrtle. Once
thought to be separate species, this changed when research
showed that they readily hybridize where ranges overlap.

Year-round | Adult female

Dendroica nigrescens L 5" (13 cm)

FIELD MARKS

Black and white head

Small yellow spot in front of eye

Gray back streaked with black;
sides streaked with black

White underparts and
undertail coverts

Behavior
Gleans insects, larvae, and caterpillars from low- to
mid-level branches, twigs, and leaves. Also is known to
hover-glean. Will occasionally give chase to flying insects
and return to perch to eat. Will join mixed-species
foraging flocks in the winter. Varied songs include a
buzzy *weezy weezy weezy weezy-weet*, with the ultimate
or penultimate note higher.

Habitat
Inhabits woodlands, brushlands, and chaparral, where
its streaked plumage serves as a sort of camouflage.
Nests alone in forks or branches of trees fairly close
to the ground. Eggs brooded by female.

Local Sites
Look for the Black-throated Gray Warbler nesting at
higher altitudes throughout the state in the summer,
especially in the coastal ranges, the Cascade-Sierra axis,
and the Warner Mountains. You may also spot it in the
winter in mixed-species foraging groups in Santa
Barbara or San Diego Counties.

FIELD NOTES The female of this species is similar to the male
but still distinguishable in the field. Look for her white chin and
throat, where the male has black feathers, and look for a gray
crown streaked with black, instead of the all-black crown of
the male.

Year-round | Adult female

TOWNSEND'S WARBLER

Dendroica townsendi L 5" (13 cm)

FIELD MARKS

Dark crown

Dark ear patch bordered in yellow

Olive above, streaked with black

Yellow breast, white belly

Sides streaked in yellowish black

Behavior

Forages and sings high in the tops of full-grown conifers. Sometimes hover-gleans for insects, caterpillars, and spiders. Song is variable but consists of a series of hoarse *zee* notes rising in pitch and dropping at end. In general, aggressive toward other species, but may join mixed foraging flocks after breeding. Both male and female build the nest and feed the nestlings, but female does the brooding.

Habitat

Found in coniferous forests of the Pacific Coast. Nests in structures of bark, plants, lichens, and grasses, built high aboveground in the limbs of tall pines and spruces. Range is increasing slightly but steadily in Washington and Oregon.

Local Sites

Keep an eye out for Townsend's Warbler along the coast, but only during the winter months.

FIELD NOTES The result of hybridization between a Hermit Warbler and a Townsend's Warbler is referred to by birders of the Pacific Northwest as a "Heto." It generally retains the yellowish, streaked underparts of the Townsend's but loses the dark crown of the Hermit, sporting instead a mostly yellow head.

Year-round | Adult male

HERMIT WARBLER

Dendroica occidentalis L 5½" (14 cm)

FIELD MARKS

Yellow head

Dark markings from nape
onto crown

Black chin and throat in male

Female chin is yellowish; throat
shows little or no dark color

Behavior

Gleans insects, caterpillars, and spiders from the upper-
most branches and leaves of conifers. Will sometimes
cling from a branch upside down to forage. Also
known to hover-glean and chase flying insects. Sings
to declare territory high up in conifers. Song is a high
seezle seezle seezle seezle zeet-zeet. Call is a dull *chip*.

Habitat

Common in mountainous forests. Female builds nest
high up in conifers with sticks, stems, lichen, hair,
feathers, and bark. Female broods eggs; both male
and female feed nestlings. Seen in lowlands only
during migration.

Local Sites

To spot the Hermit Warbler in the summer, look to
the tops of fir and pine trees dotting the slopes of the
Warner and Klamath Mountains in the north, the Cascade-Sierra Axis, or the San Gabriel, San Bernardino,
and San Jacinto Mountains in the south.

FIELD NOTES Though widespread in the tall, old-growth conifer
forests of the Pacific Northwest, the picky Hermit Warbler is at
risk of population decline because of habitat loss due to logging.
Where their ranges overlap, the Hermit is also known to be dis-
placed by the Townsend's Warbler; the two are unable to find
coexisting microhabitats without interbreeding.

Immature | Juvenile female

WILSON'S WARBLER

Wilsonia pusilla L 4¾" (12 cm)

FIELD MARKS
Olive above, yellow below with
yellow lores

Long tail, all dark above
and below

Black cap in male

Cap blackish or absent in female

Behavior
A docile and inquisitive bird. Long tail is often cocked.
Moves up and down or in a circle as it gleans spiders,
insects, and berries from foliage. Is known to hover-
glean or hawk flying insects. Song is a rapid, variable
series of *chee* notes. Common call is a sharp *chimp*.

Habitat
A fairly common bird, more numerous in the West
than East. Nests in loose colonies, for the most part
monogamously, within dense, moist woodlands, bogs,
willow thickets, and streamside tangles.

Local Sites
Look for the Wilson's Warbler nesting in the boreal
forests of the Cascade-Sierra axis, in the Klamath and
Warner Mountains to the north, and in the environs of
the San Gabriel and San Bernardino Mountains to the
south. It could be alone or with a mate.

FIELD NOTES Wilson's Warblers can be found in the Canadian
Northeast around the Gulf of St. Lawrence and the Hudson Bay,
but those have greenish-yellow underparts. More commonly—and
exclusively in California—they show bright yellow underparts.

Year-round | Adult male

COMMON YELLOWTHROAT

Geothylpis trichas L 5" (13 cm)

FIELD MARKS

Adult male shows broad, black
mask bordered above by gray

Yellow throat and breast

Yellow undertail coverts

Female lacks black mask,
has whitish eye ring

Behavior

Generally remains close to ground, skulking and
hiding in overgrowth. May also be seen climbing
vertically on stems. While foraging, hops on ground
to glean insects, caterpillars, and spiders from foliage,
twigs, and grass. Sometimes gleans while hovering, or
gives chase to flying insects.

Habitat

Stays low in grassy fields, shrubs, and marshes. Is a
solitary nester atop piles of weed and grass, or in small
shrubs. Female builds nest alone from dried grasses
and leaves, stems, pieces of bark, and hair.

Local Sites

Breeds around Tule Lake National Wildlife Reserve in
the north, over to the west coast, where Patrick's Point
State Park and Arcata Marsh and Wildlife Sanctuary
provide excellent shelter. Year round, Yellowthroats
inhabit the mid- to southern California coast.

FIELD NOTES The colors of the Yellowthroat vary widely,
according to geography. Differences reveal themselves in the
amount of yellow on the underparts, the extent of olive shading
on the upperparts, and the color of the border between mask
and crown, which can go from stark white to gray. The southwestern race, *Geothlypis trichas chryseola*, is the brightest
below and shows the most yellow.

Year-round | Adult female

YELLOW WARBLER

Dendroica petechia L 5" (13 cm)

FIELD MARKS

Bright yellow overall

Plump and short-tailed

Dark eye prominent in yellow face

Male shows distinct reddish streaks below; streaks faint or absent in female

Behavior
Forages in trees, shrubs, and bushes, gleaning insects, larvae, and fruit from their branches and leaves. Will sometimes spot flying insects from a perch and chase them down. Mostly seen by itself or in a pair. Male and female both feed nestlings, sometimes mistakenly giving them noxious, leaf-eating caterpillars. Song is a rapid, variable *sweet sweet I'm so sweet.*

Habitat
Favors wet habitats, especially those with willows and alders, but also lives in open woodlands, gardens, and orchards. Nests in the forks of trees or bushes at eye level or a little higher.

Local Sites
The Yellow Warbler is a summer visitor to all California's higher elevation ranges, including the San Rafael and San Bernardino Ranges in the southwest. Mono Lake County Park in the Sierra Nevadas is a great spot to see this plump-bodied bird.

FIELD NOTES A common victim of the cowbird invading its nest, the Yellow Warbler has devised an interesting retaliation tactic. Once foreign eggs are detected, the female will build a new roof of grasses, moss, lichen, and fur over all the eggs, then simply lay a new clutch. A single nest has been found to have up to six stories embedded with cold cowbird and warbler eggs.

Year-round | Adult male *oregonus*

SPOTTED TOWHEE

Pipilo maculatus L 7½" (19 cm)

FIELD MARKS

Black upperparts and hood

Rufous sides

White underparts

White spots on back
and scapulars

Two white wing bars

Behavior

This towhee employs its signature double-scratch as it
drags its feet along leaf litter, head held low and tail
pointed up, attempting to expose seeds, fruit, and small
arthropods, especially beetles, caterpillars, and spiders.
The Pacific Coast subspecies sings a simple trill of
variable speed from its exposed perch. Its call is an
upslurred, inquisitive *queee*.

Habitat

Common in chaparral, brushy thickets, and forest
edges. Largely resident population in California. Nests
on ground, but occasionally in low trees or shrubs.

Local Sites

Darkest subspecies, *oregonus*, lives in northern coastal
ranges. Other subspecies—*falcinellus*, a visitor to the
Central Valley, and southern Cali-
fornia's *megalonyx*—show more
white spotting on the upperparts,
wings, and under the tail.

FIELD NOTES The California Towhee, *Pipilo
crissalis* (inset), shares much of the same range and
habitat in California as the Spotted, as well as the double-
scratch feeding method, but is easily distinguished by its brownish color and its buff throat and lores. Look for the two side by
side at Ano Nuevo State Reserve, west of San Jose.

Year-round | Adults

LARK SPARROW

Chondestes grammacus L 6½" (17 cm)

FIELD MARKS

Bold head pattern of chestnut, white, and black

Whitish underparts

Dark central breast spot

White cornered tail, conspicuous in flight

Behavior

Forages in flocks for seeds, insects, and caterpillars, either on the ground or in low branches. During courtship, male swaggers on the ground and spreads his tail to show off his white feathers, then presents female with a twig or stem before copulating. A frequent singer, the Lark Sparrow vocalizes on the ground, from a perch, while flying, and often at night. Song begins with two loud, clear notes, followed by a series of rich, melodious notes and trills, then unmusical buzzes.

Habitat

Found on prairies, roadsides, farms, open woodlands, grasslands, and mesas west of the Mississippi River. Nests on grass near or in a bush, or low in a tree. Look for distraction display by female, who scurries off, wings fluttering and tail spread, if nest is disturbed.

Local Sites

Little Panoche Reservoir in the Panoche Valley of central California is a good place to spot the Lark Sparrow any time of the year.

FIELD NOTES A good way to find a Lark Sparrow is to walk softly and slowly through an open field, making a *pish* sound. Once the bird flushes, look for the distinctive chestnut, white, and black head pattern combined with the standard sparrow back streaking to identify this particular species.

Year-round | Adult *beldingi*

SAVANNAH SPARROW

Passerculus sandwichensis L 5½" (14 cm)

FIELD MARKS

Yellow or whitish eyebrow

Pale median crown stripe

Strong postocular stripe

Variable streaked upperparts

Buff to white underparts with variable streaking

Behavior

Forages on the ground for insects, spiders, and some-times snails in the summer, seeds and berries in the winter. Roosts on the ground in small, close-knit groups. When alarmed, runs through grasses on the ground instead of flying. If pressed, may fly only short distances before dropping back down into grasses. Song begins with two or three *chip* notes, then two buzzy trills. Distinctive flight call is a thin *seep*.

Habitat

Common in a variety of open habitats, marshes, and grasslands. Can be found on farm fields, meadows, golf courses, tundra, bogs, beaches, and grassy dunes. Nests in ground depressions or self-made scrapes in enclaves sheltered by vines or tall grasses.

Local Sites

Look for migrating flocks overhead in early fall and spring. Also found up and down the coast or around Mono Lake. Southern California's coastal marshes are best for spotting the *beldingi* subspecies.

FIELD NOTES On the West Coast, races of this species get increasingly darker the farther south you go. The *beldingi* of southern California's coastal marshes is the darkest. The *rostratus*, or Large-billed Sparrow, is much duller and may be seen in small numbers on the edge of the Salton Sea in winter.

Year-round | Adult *melodia*

SONG SPARROW

Melospiza melodia L 5¾-7½" (16-19 cm)

FIELD MARKS

Upperparts streaked

Underparts whitish, with streaking on sides and breast

Long, rounded tail

Broad, grayish eyebrow

Broad, dark malar stripe

Behavior
Pumps tail up and down in flight. Scratches ground with feet to unearth grain, seeds, berries, and insects. Also forages in trees and bushes and on the ground for larvae, fruits, and berries. Female broods young while male defends breeding territory intently, singing from exposed perches and battling with competitors. Typical song, though variable, is three to four short, clear notes followed by a buzzy *tow-wee* and a trill. Distinctive call is a nasal, hollow *chimp*.

Habitat
Found abundantly in suburban and rural gardens, in weedy fields, and in brushy areas, especially dense streamside thickets and forest edges. Nests on the ground or low to it in trees and bushes, hence the Song Sparrow is one of the most frequent victims of nest parasitism by the Brown-headed Cowbird.

Local Sites
Common throughout, even in towns, cities, and suburban backyard settings.

FIELD NOTES A highly variable species. Train your eye to distinguish between the *saltonis*, a paler race which inhabits parts of the deserts of southeastern California; the *morphna*, a darker, redder race in the northern coastal ranges; and the *heermanni*, a black-streaked race found rarely outside California.

Year-round | Adult *gambelii*

Zonotrichia albicollis L 7" (18 cm)

FIELD MARKS

Black-and-white striped crown

Underparts mostly gray; whitish throat and belly

Brownish upperparts with blackish brown streaking

Pink, orange, or yellowish bill

Behavior

Scratches feet along the ground, foraging to dig up insects, caterpillars, and seeds. The operation is audible in areas where wintering flocks congregate. Also gleans food from vegetation. Male sings from exposed perches to announce territory, sometimes inciting fights, and to attract females. Male feeds nestlings while female starts a new nest. Song variable by region, most often heard in winter. Usually one or more thin, whistled notes followed by a twittering trill. Calls include a loud *pink* and a sharp *tseep*.

Habitat

Generally common in woodlands, grasslands, and roadside hedges. Nests on piles of grass or moss, usually in a bush or tree.

Local Sites

Most abundant in winter, the White-crowned may still be found year-round along the Cascade-Sierra range and in the northern coastal ranges. Ano Nuevo State Reserve is a great spot to find a nesting pair.

FIELD NOTES Of the multiple subspecies, the one most encountered in the southern Cascades and the high Sierras is the *oriantha*, with a black area above the lores, and a large pink bill. In the coastal *nuttalli* and *pugetensis* subspecies, look for browner breast and back, dull yellow bill, and a pale area above the lores.

Year-round | Adult male *hyemalis*

DARK-EYED JUNCO

Junco hyemalis L 6¼" (16 cm)

FIELD MARKS

Variable dark upperparts; whitish underparts

Gray or brown head and breast, sharply set off in most races

White outer tail feathers in flight

Juveniles of all races are streaked

Behavior

Scratches on ground and forages by gleaning seeds, grain, berries, insects, caterpillars, and fruit from plants. Will occasionally give chase to a flying insect. Male gathers material for nest, which female builds. Forms flocks in winter, when larger males may travel farther north or to greater elevations than juveniles and females. Song is a musical trill that varies in pitch and tempo. Calls include a sharp *dit,* and a rapid twittering in flight.

Habitat

Breeds in coniferous or mixed woodlands, and in bogs. Winters in a wide variety of habitats throughout much of North America. Nests on or close to ground, either sheltered by a bush, or in a cavity such as a tree root.

Local Sites

Look for the Oregon Junco subspecies with a blackish hood, a buff-brown back, and a white belly, found all year along the coastal ranges, in the Cascade-Sierras, and in the Warner Mountains of northeast California.

FIELD NOTES The five different subspecies of the Dark-eyed Junco were unified under the same heading by the American Ornithologists' Union in 1973, although they are widely scattered geographically and highly disparate in their field marks. They do all share their white outer tail feathers, their song, their behavioral habits, and, most important, their genetic makeup.

Breeding | Adult male

BLACK-HEADED GROSBEAK

Pheucticus melanocephalus L 8¼" (21 cm)

FIELD MARKS

Very large, dark, triangular bill

Yellow wing linings show in flight

Male has cinnamon underparts; black head and upperparts

Female buffy above and below, with little streaking on underparts

Behavior

Forages for seeds, insects, caterpillars, berries, and fruit on the ground and in trees and bushes. In flight, beats wings rapidly in between brief periods spent gliding with its wings at sides. Rich back-and-forth warbled song, relatively low-pitched. Call is a sharp, nonsqueaky *eek*. Both male and female are known to sing at very low volumes while incubating and brooding.

Habitat

Lives in open and streamside woodlands, especially pine and pine-oak, and forest edges. Nests moderately high up in dense vegetation of trees or shrubs, usually near water. Young brooded by both male and female.

Local Sites

The Black-headed Grosbeak is a summer visitor in most of the state, except southeastern desert regions. The oak woods of Santa Barbara Botanic Garden are an ideal nesting spot.

FIELD NOTES The Black-headed Grosbeak is known to hybridize with its cousin, the Rose-breasted Grosbeak, *Pheucticus ludovicianus*, where their ranges overlap in the Great Plains. Their nearly identical songs no doubt promote the interchange. To distinguish by sight, look for a cinnamon breast, as opposed to rose-colored, in the Black-headed male, and look for a lack of heavy streaking on the breast of the Black-headed female.

Breeding | Adult

Sturnella neglecta L 9½" (24 cm)

FIELD MARKS

Black V-shaped breast band
on yellow underparts

Long, pointed bill

Lateral crown stripes

Brown tail with white stripes
on either side

Behavior

Strong, direct flight. A ground feeder with strong legs
for walking, forages through marsh edges, lakeshores,
fields, meadows, and lawns, gleaning whatever might
be available. Uses long, thin, sharp-tipped bill to pluck
and eat a variety of food including seeds, fruit, insects,
worms, mussels, and crayfish. Its call helps identify the
Western Meadowlark: a whistled *wheet*. Its song is a
series of bubbling, flutelike notes of variable length,
usually accelerating toward the end.

Habitat

Prefers the open space offered by pastures, prairies,
and farm fields. Also frequents lakeshores and
suburban lawns.

Local Sites

Ranges throughout California year-round. In winter,
large flocks gather along roadsides, unlike Eastern
Meadowlarks, which prefer taller cover.

FIELD NOTES Within their family, which includes blackbirds and
grackles, only the meadowlarks and bobolinks are true songbirds. While the song of the Eastern Meadowlark is less melodic
than that of the Western Meadowlark, both species project similarly rich, musical territorial songs that carry far across the open
grassland habitats they prefer.

Year-round | Adult male

RED-WINGED BLACKBIRD

Agelaius phoeniceus L 8¾" (22 cm)

FIELD MARKS

Male is glossy black

Red shoulder patches broadly
tipped with buffy yellow

Heavily streaked below

Female dark brown above

Behavior

The male's bright red shoulder patches are usually
visible when it sings from a perch, often atop a cattail
or tall grass stalk, defending its territory. At other times
only the yellow border may be visible. Forages for
insects, grass seeds, and agricultural grain in pastures
and open fields; sometimes is considered a threat to
crops. Call is a liquid, gurgling *konk-la-reee,* ending in
a trill. Call is a *chack* note. Breeding males often have
more than one mate, and therefore spend less time
caring for young than do the females.

Habitat

Breeds mainly in freshwater marshes with thick
vegetation. In winter, males and females flock together
and forage in wooded swamps and farm fields.

Local Sites

Year-round range is throughout California. Slight race
variations occur in the Central Valley, the central
coastal region, and the south-central Kern Basin.

FIELD NOTES The related Tricolored Blackbird, *Agelaius tricolor,*
has more pointed wings and bill than the Red-winged, and the
male's red shoulder patches are broadly tipped in white. The
Tricolored's song is a harsher *on-ke-kaaangh*. Very often the
majority of blackbirds in a large winter flock are Red-winged,
not Tricolored.

Year-round | Adult male

GREAT-TAILED GRACKLE

Quiscalus mexicanus L 18" (46 cm) Female L 15" (38 cm)

FIELD MARKS

Large grackle with very long, keel-shaped tail

Golden-yellow eyes

Male iridescent black, purple sheen on head, back, and underparts

Behavior

Not territorial, especially in areas with rich food sources. May practice polygamy: Dominant males gather a harem of females, with which they mate and whom they will defend against advances by other, lesser males. In winter, Great-tailed Grackles may join large groups, numbering in the thousands, of single or mixed species flocks. Together the flocks forage, locating rich food sources and sharing their finds. Some may flush insects or other prey. Individuals spend less time on the alert for predators, since all glance around for danger. Voices are harsh, with varied calls, including clear whistles and loud *clack* notes.

Habitat

Common in open flatlands with scattered groves of trees, and in marshes and wetlands.

Local Sites

See Great-tailed Grackles year-round in southern California. These birds breed throughout the American Southwest.

FIELD NOTES All grackle females build cup- or bowl-shaped nests, sometimes bulky and unsightly. In them, females lay four to six eggs. While most other grackle males help care for the young, Great-tailed Grackle males do not. It is strictly the female's duty.

Year-round | Adult male

BREWER'S BLACKBIRD

Euphagus cyanocephalus L 9" (23 cm)

FIELD MARKS

Male black year-round, with purplish gloss on head and neck, greenish gloss on body and wings

Bill is sharp, straight

Male has yellow eyes

Female has brown eyes, gray body

Behavior

Like all blackbirds, the Brewer's has strong legs and feet that allow it to take long walks to forage on the ground. With straight, strong, sharp-tipped bill, it eats insects, fruit, grain, and seeds. Known to assemble in parking lots to pick protein-rich insects from car grilles. Builds coarse, cup-shaped nests. Largely monogamous. Call is a harsh *check;* song a wheezy *quee-ee* or *k-seee.*

Habitat

Common in open habitats, including fields, suburbs with parks, and parking lots.

Local Sites

Year-round range is all of California, though it winters in central and southeastern California. Then Brewer's and other blackbirds can be observed in mixed flocks that include cowbirds, grackles, and starlings. Long ribbons of these several species of dark birds in flight can seem to stretch from horizon to horizon.

FIELD NOTES Strong jaw musculature allows blackbirds to close their bills forcefully—and then forcefully open them in an action called "gaping." Gaping allows the birds to pry into crevices, soft bark, dirt, and leaf litter to expose prey hidden to other birds.

Year-round | Adult male

BROWN-HEADED COWBIRD

Molothrus ater L 7½" (19 cm)

FIELD MARKS
Pointed bill

In male, brown head and metallic
green-black body

Female gray-brown above,
paler below

Strong, direct flight

Behavior
Often forages on the ground among herds of cattle,
feeding on insects flushed out by grazing. Also feeds
heavily on grass seeds and agricultural grain, and is
sometimes viewed as a threat to crops. Generally cocks
its tail up while feeding. Song is a squeaky, gurgling call
that includes a squeaky whistle. All cowbirds are nest
parasites and lay their eggs in the nests of other species,
leaving the responsibilities of feeding and fledging of
young to the host birds.

Habitat
Cowbirds prefer the open habitat provided by
farmlands, pastures, prairies, and edgelands bordering
woods and forests. Also frequent suburbs.

Local Sites
Find them throughout California year-round, spanning
the length of the state along the coast. Cowbirds breed
inland, concentrating along California's eastern border.

FIELD NOTES The Brown-headed Cowbird flourishes throughout
North America, adapting to land being cleared and exposing
new songbirds—now over 200 species—to its parasitic brooding
habit. The female lays up to 40 eggs a season in the nests of
host birds, destroying host eggs in the process and impacting
endangered species such as the Kirtland's Warbler and the
Black-capped Vireo.

Breeding | Adult male

BULLOCK'S ORIOLE

Icterus bullockii L 8¼" (22 cm)

FIELD MARKS

Bold white patch on wing

Orange underparts and outer tail feathers

Yellow throat and breast in female

Black crown, nape, eye stripe, and throat patch in breeding male

Behavior

Often hard to spot, but can be heard moving or singing. Often sits on high, exposed perches. Song is composed of whistles and harsher notes; call is a clear, harsh *cheh*, sometimes in a series. Inserts long, sharply pointed bill into crevices to probe for ants, mayflies, and spiders. In breeding season, male chases female with such actions as wing-drooping and repeated bowing, all while displaying brilliant plumage. Pairs mate for one season. Females weave grasses into intricate hanging baskets or pouches for nests.

Habitat

Frequents desert or wooded habitat, where it forages in trees and shrubs. Breeds where shade trees grow.

Local Sites

Breeds throughout state. Orioles visit suburban yards for food from feeding stations. In the arid south, they glean fruit, insects, and nectar from cactuses. Small numbers winter along coastal California.

FIELD NOTES The Bullock's Oriole was once considered to be the same species as the Baltimore Oriole, in large part because the two species interbreed, or hybridize, where their ranges overlap in the Great Plains.

Year-round | Adult male

HOUSEFINCH

Carpodacus mexicanus L 6" (15 cm)

FIELD MARKS

Male has brown cap

Front of head, bib, and rump typically red, but can be orange or, occasionally, yellow

Bib set off from streaked underparts

Female brown-streaked overall

Behavior
Active, acrobatic birds, finches are often seen spiraling overhead in large flocks of several hundred at a time, sometimes containing several species. Can hang upside-down to reach seeds or buds, in contrast to buntings and sparrows, which forage on the ground. Will visit bird feeders when natural sources are scarce. Lively, high-pitched song, usually ending in a nasal *wheer*. Calls include a whistled *wheat*.

Habitat
Varied, including woodlands, tundra, and city parks, as well as dry, nearly desertlike climates.

Local Sites
Seen throughout California year-round in cities, suburbs, and populated agricultural areas. Also inhabits semiarid lowlands and slopes up to about 6,000 feet. Especially abundant in towns in its native range, the western United States and Mexico.

FIELD NOTES The Purple Finch, *Carpodacus purpureus* (inset), is not purple but rose-red over most of the adult male's body. The brown female is heavily streaked below. This Pacific Coast race frequents canyons, forests, and mountain slopes.

Breeding | Adult male

AMERICAN GOLDFINCH

Carduelis tristis L 5" (13 cm)

FIELD MARKS

Male bright yellow with black cap; female duller overall, lacks cap

Black wings have white bars; male has yellow shoulder patch

White uppertail and undertail coverts

Behavior

Gregarious and active, often seen spiraling overhead as it travels in flocks during nonbreeding season. Flocks may contain a hundred or more birds and include several species. Distinctive flight call is *per-chik-o-ree.* An acrobatic forager, it hangs upside down to reach seeds or buds. May visit birdfeeders when natural food is scarce. The finch diet, heavily seeds and vegetable matter, is the most vegetarian of any North American bird, but this bird sometimes does eat insects. Song is a lively series of trills, twitters, and *swee* notes.

Habitat

Found in weedy fields, open second-growth wood-lands, and on roadsides. Especially seeks territory rich in thistles and sunflowers.

Local Sites

Year-round range extends along the California coast. In winter find it inland, in the arid California south.

FIELD NOTES Slightly smaller than the American Goldfinch, the Lesser Goldfinch, *Carduelis psaltria* (inset), is identified by an all-black crown and deep green back. Its relative has a black cap and yellow back.

Mostly Black

 Double-crested Cormorant, 48

 Brandt's Cormorant, 50

 Turkey Vulture, 60

 American Coot, 76

 Black Oystercatcher, 82

 American Crow, 174

 European Starling, 214

 Red-winged Blackbird, 248

 Great-tailed Grackle, 250

 Brewer's Blackbird, 252

 Brown-headed Cowbird, 254

 Black-bellied Plover, 78

 Black Turnstone, 94

 White-throated Swift, 134

 Acorn Woodpecker, 146

 White-headed Woodpecker, 148

 Nuttall's Woodpecker, 154

 Downey Woodpecker, 156

 Black Phoebe, 162

 Black-billed Magpie, 172

Mostly Black and Gray

 Black-crowned Night-Heron, 52

Mostly Black and White

 Lesser Scaup, 24

 Surf Scoter, 26

 Bufflehead, 28

 Common Loon, 36

 Horned Grebe, 40

 Western Grebe, 44

Mostly Black and Brown

 American Avocet, 84

 Spotted Towhee, 232

Mostly Brown and White

 Canada Goose, 12

 Northern Pintail, 22

Osprey, 62

Killdeer, 80

Least Sandpiper, 98

Mostly Blue

Belted Kingfisher, 144

Steller's Jay, 166

Western Scrub-Jay, 168

Island Scrub-Jay, 170

Tree Swallow, 178

Barn Swallow, 180

Western Bluebird, 206

Mostly Brown

American Wigeon, 14

Cinnamon Teal, 18

Ruddy Duck, 32

California Quail, 34

Brown Pelican, 46

Pied-billed Grebe, 42

Golden Eagle, 68

Red-tailed Hawk, 72

American Kestrel, 74

Greater Yellowlegs, 88

Long-billed Curlew, 90

Marbled Godwit, 92

Long-billed Dowitcher, 100

Mourning Dove, 120

Barn Owl, 122

Short-eared Owl, 124

Great-horned Owl, 126

Burrowing Owl, 130

Common Nighthawk, 132

Rufous Hummingbird, 140

Northern Flicker, 150

Horned Lark, 176

House Wren, 190

Winter Wren, 192

Bewick's Wren, 194

Cactus Wren, 196

Rock Wren, 198

Marsh Wren, 200

American Robin, 208

California Thrasher, 212

Cedar Waxwing, 216

Lark Sparrow, 234

Savannah Sparrow, 236

Song Sparrow, 238

White-crowned Sparrow, 240

Mostly Gray

Red-throated Loon, 38

Great Blue Heron, 58

Northern Harrier, 66

Cooper's Hawk, 70

Willet, 86

Sanderling, 96

Heermann's Gull, 104

Rock Pigeon, 118

Western Screech-Owl, 128

Western Wood-Pewee, 160

Oak Titmouse, 182

Mountain Chickadee, 184

Bushtit, 186

White-breasted Nuthatch, 188

American Dipper, 202

Golden-crowned Kinglet, 204

Northern Mockingbird, 210

Black-throated Gray Warbler, 220

Dark-eyed Junco, 242

Prominent Green Heads

Mallard, 16

Northern Shoveler, 20

Red-breasted Merganser, 30

Mostly Green

Green Heron, 54

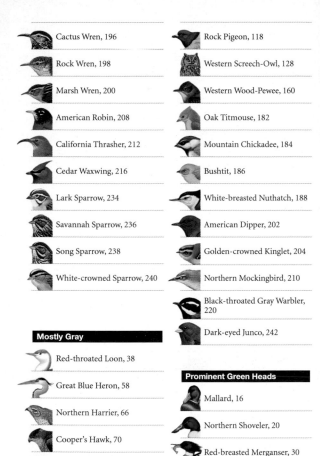

Black-chinned Hummingbird, 136

 Anna's Hummingbird, 138

 Allen's Hummingbird, 142

 Pacific-slope Flycatcher, 158

Prominent Orange

 Black-headed Grosbeak, 244

 Bullock's Oriole, 256

Mostly Red

 Red-breasted Sapsucker, 152

 House Finch, 258

Mostly White

 Snow Goose, 10

 Great Egret, 56

 White-tailed Kite, 64

 Red-necked Phalarope, 102

Bonaparte's Gull, 106

Mew Gull, 108

 California Gull, 110

 Ring-billed Gull, 112

 Caspian Tern, 114

 Forster's Tern, 116

Mostly Yellow

 Western Kingbird, 164

 Wilson's Warbler, 226

 Common Yellowthroat, 228

 Yellow Warbler, 230

Western Meadowlark, 246

Black and Yellow

 Yellow-rumped Warbler, 218

 Townsend's Warbler, 222

 Hermit Warbler, 224

 American Goldfinch, 260

The main entry for each species is listed in **boldface** type and refers to the text page opposite the illustration.

A check-off box is provided next to each common-name entry so that you can use this index as a checklist of the species you have identified.

❏ **A**vocet, American **85**

Blackbird
❏ Brewer's **253**
❏ Red-winged **249**
❏ Tricolored **249**
Bluebird
❏ Mountain **207**
❏ Western **207**
❏ Bufflehead **29**
❏ Bushtit **187**

Chickadee
❏ Chestnut-backed **185**
❏ Mountain **185**
Coot
❏ American **77**
Cormorant
❏ Brandt's **51**
❏ Double-crested **49**
❏ Pelagic **51**
Cowbird
❏ Brown-headed **255**
Crow
❏ American **175**
Curlew
❏ Long-billed **91**

Dipper
❏ American **203**
Dove
❏ Common Ground **121**
❏ Mourning **121**

❏ Rock **119**
Dowitcher
❏ Long-billed **101**
❏ Short-billed **101**
Duck
❏ Ruddy **33**
❏ Dunlin **97**

Eagle
❏ Bald **69**
❏ Golden **69**
Egret
❏ Great **57**
❏ Snowy **57**

Falcon
❏ Peregrine **75**
❏ Prairie **75**
Finch
❏ House **259**
❏ Purple **259**
Flicker
❏ Northern **151**
Flycatcher
❏ Olive-sided **161**
❏ Pacific-slope **159**

Godwit
❏ Marbled **93**
Goldfinch
❏ American **261**
❏ Lesser **261**
Goose
❏ Canada **13**
❏ Ross's **11**
❏ Snow **11**
Grackle
❏ Great-tailed **251**
Grebe
❏ Clark's **45**
❏ Eared **41**
❏ Horned **41, 43**
❏ Pied-billed **43**
❏ Western **45**
Grosbeak

❏ Black-headed 245
Gull
❏ Bonaparte's 196, 212
❏ California 200, 213
❏ Heermann's 194
❏ Herring 202, 213
❏ Mew 198, 212
❏ Ring-billed 198, 212

Harrier
❏ Northern 67
Hawk
❏ Cooper's 71
❏ Red-shouldered 73
❏ Red-tailed 73
Heron *see also* Night-Heron
❏ Great Blue 59
❏ Green 55
Hummingbird
❏ Allen's 143
❏ Anna's 139
❏ Black-chinned 137
❏ Costa's 139
❏ Rufous 141

Jay
❏ Island Scrub- 171
Scrub *see* Jay, Island Scrub-;
Jay, Western Scrub-
❏ Steller's 167
❏ Western Scrub- 169
Junco
❏ Dark-eyed 243

Kestrel
❏ American 75
❏ Killdeer 81
Kingbird
❏ Western 165
Kingfisher
❏ Belted 145
Kinglet
❏ Golden-crowned 205
❏ Ruby-crowned 205

Kite
❏ White-tailed 64
Black-shouldered 64

Lark
❏ Horned 177
Loon
❏ Common 37
❏ Pacific 39
❏ Red-throated 39

Magpie
❏ Black-billed 173
❏ Yellow-billed 173
❏ Mallard 17
Meadowlark
❏ Western 247
Merganser
❏ Common 31
❏ Red-breasted 31
Mockingbird
❏ Northern 211
❏ Moorhen, Common 77

Night-Heron
❏ Black-crowned 53
Nighthawk
❏ Common 133
❏ Lesser 133
Nuthatch
❏ Pygmy 189
❏ Red-breasted 189
❏ White-breasted 189

Oriole
❏ Bullock's 257
❏ Osprey 63
Owl
❏ Barn 123
❏ Burrowing 131
❏ Great Horned 127
❏ Long-eared 125
❏ Short-eared 125
❏ Western Screech- 129

Oystercatcher
❏   Black 83

Pelican
❏   American White 47
❏   Brown 47
Pewee
❏   Cuban 286
❏   Eastern Wood- 286
❏   Greater 286
❏   Western Wood- 161
Phalarope
❏   Red-necked 103
❏   Wilson's 103
Phoebe
❏   Black 163
Pigeon
❏   Rock 119
Pintail
❏   Northern 23
Plover
❏   Black-bellied 79

Quail
❏   California 35
❏   Gambel's 35

Raven
❏   Common 175
Robin
❏   American 209

Sanderling 97
Sandpiper
❏   Least 99
❏   Western 99
Sapsucker
❏   Red-breasted 153
Scaup
❏   Greater 25
❏   Lesser 25
Scoter
❏   Surf 27
❏   White-winged 27
❏ Shoveler, Northern 21

Shrike
❏   Loggerhead 211
Sparrow
❏   House 263
❏   Lark 235
❏   Savannah 237
❏   Song 239
❏   White-crowned 241
❏ Starling, European 215
❏ Stilt, Black-necked 85
Swallow
❏   Barn 181
❏   Cliff 181
❏   Northern Rough-winged 181
❏   Tree 179
❏   Violet-green 179
Swift
❏   White-throated 135

Teal
❏   Cinnamon 19
❏   Green-winged 21
Tern
❏   Caspian 115
❏   Elegant 115
❏   Forster's 117
❏   Royal 115
Thrasher
❏   California 213
Thrush
❏   Hermit 209
❏   Varied 209
Titmouse
❏   Juniper 183
❏   Oak 183
Towhee
❏   California 233
❏   Spotted 233
❏ Turkey, Wild 132
Turnstone
❏   Black 95
❏   Ruddy 95

❏ **V**erdin 187

Vulture
❏ Turkey 67

Warbler
❏ Black-throated Gray 221
❏ Hermit 225
❏ Townsend's 223
❏ Wilson's 227
❏ Yellow 231
❏ Yellow-rumped 219
Waxwing
❏ Cedar 217
❏ Whimbrel 91
Wigeon
❏ American 15
❏ Willet 87
Woodpecker
❏ Acorn 147
❏ Downy 157
❏ Gila 147
❏ Hairy 157
❏ Ladder-backed 155
❏ Nuttall's 155
❏ White-headed 149
Wren
❏ Bewick's 195
❏ Cactus 197
❏ House 191
❏ Marsh 201
❏ Rock 199
❏ Winter 193
❏ Wrentit 187

Yellowlegs
❏ Greater 89
❏ Lesser 89
Yellowthroat
❏ Common 388
❏ Gray-crowned 388

ACKNOWLEDGMENTS

The Book Division would like to thank the following people for their guidance and contribution in creating the *National Geographic Field Guide to Birds: California*

Cortez C. Austin, Jr.:
Cortez Austin is a wildlife photographer who specializes in North American and tropical birds. His photographs feature birds sought after by scientists and birders alike. An ardent conservationist, he has donated images, given lectures and written book reviews for conservation organizations. He has published articles and photographs in birding magazines in the United States. His photographs have also appeared in field guides, books, and brochures on wildlife.

Bates Littlehales:
National Geographic photographer for more than 30 years covering myriad subjects around the globe, Bates Littlehales continues to specialize in photographing birds and is an expert in capturing their beauty and ephemeral nature. Bates is co-author of the *National Geographic Field Guide to Photography: Birds,* and a contributor to the *National Geographic Reference Atlas to the Birds of North America.*

Rulon Simmons:
Co-author of the *National Geographic Field Guide to Photography: Birds,* with Bate Littlehales, Rulon Simmons is a technical expert with Eastman Kodak, in which he works with imaging systems for aircraft and satellites. Combining this skill with his passion for birding, he photographs species across North America.

Brian Sullivan:
Birding travels and field projects have taken Brian Sullivan to Central and South America, to the Arctic and across North America during the past 12 years. He has written and consulted on various books, and on popular, and scientific literature on North American birds. Research interests include migration, seabirds, raptors and bird identification. He is currently a PRBO Field Coordinator for the endangered San Clemente Loggerhead Shrike Recovery Project.

Tom Vezo:
Tom Vezo is an award-winning wildlife photographer who is widely published throughout the U.S. and Europe. He specializes in bird photography but photographs other wildlife and nature subjects as well. He is a contributor to the *National Geographic Reference Atlas to the Birds of North America.* Please visit Tom at his website www.tomvezo.com.

Cover George Mobley; 2 Brian Sullivan; 10 Rulon Simmons; 12 Cortez C.
Austin Jr.; 14 Cortez C. Austin Jr.; 16 Bates Littlehales; 18 Rulon Simmons;
20 Bates Littlehales; 22 Rulon Simmons; 24 Cortez C. Austin Jr.; 26 Bates
Littlehales; 28 Rulon Simmons; 30 Bates Littlehales; 32 Bates Littlehales;
34 Rulon Simmons; 36 Kennan Ward/CORBIS; Paul Nicklen, National
Geographic Image Collection; 40 Tom Vezo; 42 Cortez C. Austin Jr.;
44 Rulon Simmons; 46 Arthur Morris/CORBIS; 48 Bates Littlehales;
50 Tom Vezo; 52 Bates Littlehales; 54 Peter Wallack; 56 Cortez C. Austin Jr.;
58 Bates Littlehales; 60 Bates Littlehales; 62 Cortez C. Austin Jr.; 64 Brian
Sullivan; 66 Ron Austing; Frank Lane Picture Agency/CORBIS; 68 Robert
Pickett/CORBIS; 70 Eric and David Hosking/CORBIS; 72 Cortez C. Austin
Jr.; 74 Joe McDonald/CORBIS; 76 Cortez C. Austin Jr.; 78 Tim
Zurowski/CORBIS; 80 Bates Littlehales; 82 Bates Littlehales; 84 Bates
Littlehales; 86 Bates Littlehales; 88 Bates Littlehales; 90 Rulon Simmons;
92 Bates Littlehales; 94 Rulon Simmons; 96 Bates Littlehales; 98 Rulon
Simmons; 100 Bates Littlehales; 102 Bates Littlehales; 104 Rulon Simmons;
106 Bates Littlehales; 108 Theo Allofs/CORBIS; 110 Bates Littlehales; 112
Cortez C. Austin Jr.; 114 George D. Lepp/CORBIS; 116 Cortez C. Austin Jr.;
118 Cortez C. Austin Jr.; 120 Cortez C. Austin Jr.; 122 Bates Littlehales;
124 Sam Abell; 126 Bates Littlehales; 128 Cortez C. Austin Jr.; 130 Bates
Littlehales; 132 Bates Littlehales; 134 Brian Sullivan; 136 Darrell
Gulin/CORBIS; 138 Brian Sullivan; 140 Tom Vezo; 142 Brian Sullivan;
144 Bates Littlehales; 146 Cortez C. Austin Jr.; 148 Tim Zurowski/CORBIS;
150 Cortez C. Austin Jr.; 152 David A. Northcott/CORBIS; 154 George D.
Lepp/CORBIS; 156 Cortez C. Austin Jr.; 158 Brian Sullivan; 160 George D.
Lepp/CORBIS; 162 Cortez C. Austin Jr.; 164 Brian Sullivan; 166 Joe
McDonald/CORBIS; 168 Cortez C. Austin Jr.; 170 Galen Rowell/CORBIS;
172 Darrell Gulin/CORBIS; 174 Cortez C. Austin Jr.; 176 Bates Littlehales;
178 Bates Littlehales; 180 Cortez C. Austin Jr.; 182 John Watkins/CORBIS;
184 Tim Zurowski/CORBIS; 186 Brian Sullivan; 188 Bates Littlehales;
190 Cortez C. Austin Jr.; 192 Tom Vezo; 194 Tom Vezo; 196 Bates
Littlehales; 198 Tom Vezo; 200 Bates Littlehales; 202 Bates Littlehales;
204 Tim Zurowski/CORBIS; 206 Cortez C. Austin Jr.; 208 Bates Littlehales;
210 Bates Littlehales; 212 Mathew Tekulsky; 214 Cortez C. Austin Jr.;
216 Cortez C. Austin Jr.; 218 Brian Sullivan; 220 Brian Sulivan; 222 Tim
Zurkowski/CORBIS; 224 Brian Sullivan; 226 Bates Littlehales; 228 Bates
Littlehales; 230 Gary W. Carter/CORBIS; 232 Darrell Gulin/CORBIS;
234 Bates Littlehales; 236 Rulon Simmons; 238 Cortez C. Austin Jr.;
240 Bates Littlehales; 242 Cortez C. Austin Jr.; 244 Cortez C. Austin Jr.;
246 Rulon Simmons; 248 Bates Littlehales; 250 D. Robert & Lorri
Franz/CORBIS; 252 Rulon Simmons; 254 Cortez C. Austin Jr.; 256 Rulon
Simmons; 258 Bates Littlehales; 260 Bates Littlehales; 262 Bates Littlehales

NATIONAL GEOGRAPHIC
FIELD GUIDE TO BIRDS:
CALIFORNIA

Edited by Mel Baughman

Published by
the National Geographic Society

John M. Fahey, Jr.,
President and Chief Executive Officer

Gilbert M. Grosvenor,
Chairman of the Board

Nina D. Hoffman,
Executive Vice President

Prepared by the Book Division

Kevin Mulroy,
Vice President and Editor-in-Chief

Charles Kogod, *Illustrations Director*

Marianne R. Koszorus, *Design Director*

Barbara Brownell Grogan,
Executive Editor

Staff for this Book

Barbara Brownell Grogan, *Editor*

Carol Norton, *Art Director*

Melissa Farris, *Design Consultant*

Sharon Berry, *Illustrations Editor*

Dan O'Toole, Mary Jo Slazak, *Writers*

Susan Tyler Hitchcock, *Text Editor*

Carl Mehler, *Director of Maps*

Mel Baughman, Matt Chwastyk,
Dan O'Toole, *Mapping Specialists,*
Map Research and Production

Rick Wain, *Production Project Manager*

Manufacturing and Quality Control

Christopher A. Liedel,
Chief Financial Officer

Phillip L. Schlosser, *Managing Director*

John T. Dunn, *Technical Director*

One of the world's largest nonprofit scientific and educational organizations, the National Geographic Society was founded in 1888 "for the increase and diffusion of geographic knowledge." Fulfilling this mission, the Society educates and inspires millions every day through its magazines, books, television programs, videos, maps and atlases, research grants, the National Geographic Bee, teacher workshops, and innovative classroom materials. The Society is supported through membership dues, charitable gifts, and income from the sale of its educational products. This support is vital to National Geographic's mission to increase global understanding and promote conservation of our planet through exploration, research, and education.

For more information, please call 1-800-NGS LINE (647-5463) or write to the following address:

National Geographic Society
1145 17th Street N.W.
Washington, D.C. 20036-4688 U.S.A.

Visit the Society's Web site at
www.nationalgeographic.com.

Library of Congress
Cataloging-in-Publication Data

Available upon request.